I*rresistible* EVANGELISM

| Steve | Dave | Doug |
| Sjogren | Ping | Pollock |

Loveland, Colorado

Group's R.E.A.L. Guarantee® to you:

This Group resource incorporates our R.E.A.L. approach to ministry—one that encourages long-term retention and life transformation. It's ministry that's:

Relational
Because learner-to-learner interaction enhances learning and builds Christian friendships.

Experiential
Because what learners experience through discussion and action sticks with them up to 9 times longer than what they simply hear or read.

Applicable
Because the aim of Christian education is to equip learners to be both hearers and doers of God's Word.

Learner-based
Because learners understand and retain more when the learning process takes into consideration how they learn best.

Irresistible Evangelism

Copyright © 2004 Steve Sjogren, Dave Ping, Doug Pollock

Visit our Web site: **www.grouppublishing.com**

CREDITS

Development Editor: *Paul Woods*	Cover Art Director/Designer: *Jeff A. Storm*
Chief Creative Officer: *Joani Schultz*	Cover Photographer: *Josh Fletcher*
Assistant Editor: *Alison Imbriaco*	Illustrator: *Matt Wood*
Book Designer: *Jean Bruns*	Production Manager: *Peggy Naylor*
Print Production Artist: *Tracy Hindman*	

Photos on pp. 91-105 courtesy of Love Abbotsford in Abbotsford, British Columbia, Canada with special thanks to Kevin Boese. Unless otherwise noted, Scripture taken from the HOLY BIBLE, NEW INTERNATIONAL VERSION®. Copyright © 1973, 1978, 1984 by International Bible Society. Used by permission of Zondervan Publishing House. All rights reserved.

LIBRARY OF CONGRESS CATALOGING-IN-PUBLICATION DATA
Sjogren, Steve, 1955-
Irresistible evangelism : natural ways to open others to Jesus / by Steve Sjogren, Dave Ping, Doug Pollock.-- 1st American pbk. ed.
   p. cm.
  Includes bibliographical references.
   ISBN 0-7644-2626-5 (pbk.)
   1. Evangelicalism. I. Ping, Dave. II. Pollock, Doug, 1957- III. Title.
BR1640.S57 2003
269'.2--dc22
                                   2003017339

10 9 8 7 6 5 4 3 2 1   13 12 11 10 09 08 07 06 05 04
Printed in the United States of America.

Irresistible EVANGELISM

STEVE: *To Jack, the best servant evangelist I know*

DAVE: *To Merry, Mary, Isabel, Chuck, and the rest of the Talawanda God Squad*

DOUG: *To David and Jonathan, in hopes that you will someday become irresistible evangelists*

English author William Makepeace Thackeray said, "'Tis not the dying for a faith that's so hard…'tis the living up to it that is difficult." We want to express our deep gratitude to the many friends, colleagues, and family members who have lived out the love of Jesus before our eyes. They have been our teachers, and they've shown us that it is possible to give away God's love, day in and day out, while coping with all of the mundane and complex pressures of living. In many ways they are the true authors of this book.

First and foremost, our thanks go to our wives. *Irresistible Evangelism* would never have appeared in print if not for the constant loving support of Janie Sjogren, Pam Ping, and Martha Pollock. They not only put up with our bad habits and long hours, but also contributed many of our best ideas and gave lots of invaluable editorial advice. There is no way to adequately express our thanks for all they do for us, but we intend to spend the rest of our lives trying.

We also wish to give special thanks to Anne Clippard, Michael and Linda Toy, and Mikal Keefer for encouraging us to pursue this project in the first place. Thanks also to Tim and Jan Johnson, Charlene Lindner, Bob and Pauline Benedict, Roy and Jacqueline Sweeny, Ernest and Sharon Doering, Craig Spinks, the supporters of the National Christian Foundation, and the many friends of Equipping Ministries International who provided the much-needed tangible support that allowed the development of the book and its companion training course.

We want to specially recognize Dave Workman, Chuck Mancini, Steve Bowen, and all of the past and present staff and volunteers at the Vineyard Community Church, as well as many friends around the world who have breathed life into servant evangelism.

Thanks also to the staff and board of Equipping Ministries International and Athletes in Action for a wide variety of help in developing and piloting the ideas that make up the bulk of this book. We love you guys! Thanks also belong to our editor Paul Woods, and the excellent team at Group Publishing for a job well done. We are also very grateful to Dr. Jean Coakley (Dave's mom) for tracking down some of the more difficult sources in the copy-editing process.

Finally, we thank God for the opportunity to share these simple words and ideas. We pray that the Holy Spirit will empower all your evangelistic efforts with his irresistible presence!

Steve Sjogren • Dave Ping • Doug Pollock

A Fresh Outlook on EVANGELISM

> "Our whole being...is one vast need...crying out for Him who can untie things that are now knotted together and tie up things that are still dangling loose."
> —C.S. Lewis,
> *The Four Loves*

> "But I, when I am lifted up from the earth, will draw all men to myself."
> —Jesus Christ,
> John 12:32

Most Christians want to see the people around them make faith commitments to Christ. Some are still desperately looking for ways to become more effective at the task, but many more have just given up.

We have joined forces to provide some practical help and encouragement to all who have even the faintest desire to introduce fellow human beings to a relationship with Jesus. As you will see, our book reflects the unique personalities and perspectives of its three authors. And we hope it will also present a fresh outlook on how we can best draw people to the One who means so much to us.

Irresistible Evangelism is designed to appeal to almost every personality type. No matter how you feel about evangelism, it will help you see evangelism in a new and friendly light. If you have thought of evangelism as awkward or obnoxious, you'll find it can be done fluently and enjoyably. You'll also find many new, ready-to-walk-out-the-door-and-use ideas.

THREE AMIGOS

Before we go into detail about the big ideas behind this book, it's important that you understand where we're coming from. We are Steve Sjogren, Dave Ping, and Doug Pollock, otherwise known as the three amigos of irresistible evangelism. The three of us have much in common. In fact, we were all born in November in three consecutive years. We had similar misspent childhoods watching way too much TV and creatively causing much vexation to our respective parents and teachers and the hardworking authority figures charged with channeling our natural orneriness toward good instead of evil.

Although we all came to faith in Christ from nonevangelical backgrounds, we have (somewhat miraculously) become leaders in our individual fields and have enjoyed being well-received conference speakers for evangelical church and parachurch audiences. None of us is content to be just a theorist or an armchair quarterback. We are passionate practitioners and hands-on "equippers," each with his own international experience and special expertise in key aspects of evangelism.

Steve Sjogren

STEVE has been motivated to practice evangelism since he came to Christ while attending college in a small town near the Arctic Circle in Norway. He came back to the United States and helped found the Southern California Vineyard movement during its early days of massive fruitfulness. For the last twenty years, he has pursued his passion for church planting and helped the Vineyard

Community Church in Cincinnati grow from an initial meeting of thirty-seven people to well over six thousand per week. He has written several books on church planting, evangelism, and church growth, and he regularly leads international conferences on these subjects.

Dave Ping

DAVE left his job as a public school teacher more than twenty-three years ago to enter a full-time ministry of counseling and evangelistic outreach to inner-city families and troubled youth. As a city director of Youth for Christ, he took all the training he could find about leading hurting people to Christ. One day he stumbled across a course that taught Christians how to use the power of listening to open hearts to Jesus,[1] and he was hooked. Since then, Dave has been passionate about equipping Christians to experience and share the abundant life Jesus promises in John 10:10.

Now Dave calls himself an evangelist to Christians. As director of Equipping Ministries International, Dave—with the help of hundreds of volunteers—has equipped more than one hundred thousand ministry staff, missionaries, and lay leaders to become more fruitful in ministry. His message is simple: *We* can actually have all the good things we've been telling others *they* could have if they would just come to Jesus! Most people won't believe Christ's promises until they see convincing evidence in *our* families, relationships, and professional lives. Evangelism is much more than just getting people to pray a prayer; but Christ's liberating message gets through when we listen, speak truth in love, and free ourselves from all the shame-producing beliefs that ruin our lives.

Doug Pollock

DOUG made a faith commitment to Christ as a junior in college and now serves as the evangelism director for Athletes in Action. During the past twenty years in sports ministry, his travels have taken him to thirty-five countries (and he's only gotten sick once!), and he's spoken on hundreds of college and high school campuses across the

United States. His passion to see people experience new life in Christ has compelled him to try out and evaluate just about every possible approach to evangelism. He has reached the conclusion that most of our methods for sharing the good news leave both Christians and pre-Christians with bad tastes in their mouths.

All three of us are more than a little bit out of the ordinary in our teaching and writing styles. We are extremely visual and intuitive. We are among the 8 percent or so of computer users who can't live without our Apple I books or PowerBooks because they "think" more like we do. To feel really confident when we speak, we need a good supply of video clips, PowerPoint slides, and music selections to enhance our teaching. We like movies better than books, and we like picture books and storybooks much better than textbooks! As a consequence, *Irresistible Evangelism* will make use of a variety of word pictures, charts, and graphs.

BEYOND SERVANT EVANGELISM

At Vineyard Community Church in Cincinnati, a simple mission statement is sandblasted into the front of the building in four-foot letters: "Small things done with great love will change the world." For more than sixteen years, all three of us have tried to put these simple words into practice in our city and around the world. Steve and his colleagues at VCC helped to pioneer the practice of servant evangelism[2] by providing more than three hundred creative ways Christians can serve and love the people around them into relationship with Jesus Christ.

More than one hundred thousand church leaders and lay people have joined this "conspiracy of kindness" during the last ten years and have used hundreds of wild ideas to touch millions of lives in the name of Jesus. The conferences, books, Web sites, and international movement that grew from this simple idea have motivated legions of previously timid Christians to step out boldly in Christ's name. All of this is great, but we believe God has much more in mind.

Many leaders who have tried and loved servant evangelism are asking, "What's next? What do we do for people *after* we give them a soft drink or wash their cars for free? Once people begin turning toward our acts of kindness, how can we help them turn toward and embrace the love of God?"

It is now clear that we need to provide a practical understanding of how to respond to the natural processes and relational power set in motion by genuine acts of kindness.

Serving people in small ways has always been just the beginning! *Irresistible Evangelism* updates what we've learned about what really works (and what doesn't) in sixteen years of practicing servant evangelism, and it explains the natural next steps in using the "gravity of love" to help draw people irresistibly toward their Creator. This book will help you if you are a pastor or a leader looking for fresh, effective outreach strategies that really work in today's rapidly changing world.

If you've tried servant evangelism and don't know what to do next, this book will provide clear principles and a practical road map for you and your people to follow. If you're a church or parachurch leader committed to evangelism but experiencing a dwindling response rate using tried-and-true evangelistic methods of the past, you'll find a fresh, holistic approach that will make a big difference. If you want to motivate and equip church members who are fearful and naturally gun-shy about evangelism, you'll find creative ways to communicate a new vision to help them reach their community, friends, and families with genuinely good news.

We'll discuss new concepts, such as how to find a person's *spiritual address*, or where the person lives, spiritually speaking. We'll compare the stages of evangelistic relationships to playing golf, the natural progressions of farming, and even to the supernatural work of angelic messengers. We'll tell lots of personal stories about our evangelistic successes and failures and about the convictions we've picked up along the way.

What we won't do is present another preset, cookie-cutter program for evangelism. Instead of a cookbook filled with our favorite evangelism recipes, we'll provide a *how-to-cook* book that lays out timeless principles you can adjust and use to lead people toward Jesus in the ever-changing cultural landscape in which you find yourself.

On that note, let's get cooking!

ENDNOTES

1. The course was developed by Equipping Ministries International. Its key concepts and skills have been updated and made into a popular seminar and accompanying book titled *Listening for Heaven's Sake*, available through EMI's Web site, www.equipmin.org.

2. The revolutionary evangelistic ideas of servant evangelism are detailed in a special tenth anniversary edition of *Conspiracy of Kindness*, available through servantevangelism.com.

CHAPTER 1

Practically IRRESISTIBLE

> "'Are you not thirsty?'
> said the Lion.
> 'I'm dying of thirst,' said Jill.
> 'Then drink,' said the Lion."
>
> —C.S. LEWIS,
> *The Silver Chair*

> "But whoever drinks the water
> I give him will never thirst.
> Indeed, the water I give him
> will become in him a spring of
> water welling up to eternal
> life."
>
> —JESUS CHRIST,
> JOHN 4:14

Early in the twentieth century, French painter Georges Rouault gave people a new way to see Jesus. Using layer upon layer of luminous colors and bold black lines, he brought biblical themes to life on his canvases, and his shockingly powerful images expressed his profound personal faith in a living Jesus. Though highly skilled and trained in the popular styles of his day, he turned his back on artistic fashion to provide fresh perspective. Because Rouault saw beyond the accepted pictures of

Christianity, he exhibited his work with other creative, cutting-edge rebels. His incandescent images of Christ healing the lame and feeding the poor were (and still are) hung side by side with landscapes by Henri Matisse and abstracts by Pablo Picasso and Georges Braque.

During his sixty years as a working artist, Rouault depicted many subjects, but his favorite by far was the face of Jesus. His studio overflowed with hundreds and hundreds of portraits of Christ. When asked why he was so obsessed with painting Jesus, his answer was simple yet remarkable. "My life's goal is to paint a portrait of Christ so moving that whoever looks on it will be immediately converted."

It sounds a little crazy, but Rouault's magnificent obsession is what this book is all about. We are writing to people who are obsessed with portraying Christ and his love in ways that are so true and so compelling that they are *irresistible*.[1] Not only do we believe that making God's message irresistible is possible and practical, we also believe that God has fashioned our hearts to receive his message.

THE GRAVITY OF LOVE

A warm, soft bed at the end of an exhausting workday; an ice-cold glass of water on a sweltering summer afternoon; the tiny, trembling fingers of a newborn infant—these are a few of the things that are simply irresistible to most people. They appeal directly to powerful needs that God designed into each human being. He made us to hunger for comfort and refreshment and to thirst for love. These God-given urges compel us in a way that mere words never could.

While the Pharisees spent most of their time disputing the meanings of words, Jesus ministered directly to people's needs. He recognized them and invited himself to dinner in their homes. He fed them, served them, and healed their sons, daughters, and mothers. As Jesus ate with them, drank with them, and mended their wounds, he told stories and asked questions that awakened a deep, supernatural thirst within them—a thirst only living water could quench. Jesus' love beckoned to people and drew them closer to God with a spiritual power as basic as gravity. This book is dedicated to the proposition that this same irresistible power is available in us today.

Poet Louis Ginsberg once said, "Love is the irresistible desire to be desired irresistibly." We all long to feel, taste, and touch unselfish, unconditional love. The longing is part of our spiritual DNA. In a world filled with disappointment, fear, and cynicism, negative forces often muffle but never completely drown out the heavenly Father's call into love. It is always there in the background, waiting to be amplified and clarified by touch—the touch of God's people. When touches bearing God's mercy and kindness get through, mysterious and wonderful transformations begin to take place.

> *"Love is metaphysical gravity."*
> —R. Buckminster Fuller

This book is for anyone who wants to learn how to genuinely love friends, family members, and even strangers into a more intimate and life-transforming relationship with Jesus Christ—without being pushy, manipulative, or obnoxious. It's a step-by-step guide to practicing simple, organic principles of what might be called spiritual gardening. We believe that, just as the right combination of sunlight, soil, and water causes seeds to grow, the proper combination of God's Spirit with simple, consistent, loving actions will cause hearts to open to Jesus. The *Irresistible Evangelism* approach seeks to recognize and activate the basic inner yearnings and spiritual receptivity that God has built into the hearts of *all* people.

DÉJÀ VU

As we write this book, headlines announce stories that echo the Crusades of the Middle Ages. Holy wars are being declared against Christianity and Western culture by leaders who promote violence to revive the Islamic golden age of the eleventh century—leaders who'd like to take Jerusalem back from the "infidels." Jihad and military crusades are being planned and executed. Battles are being fought, and more battle lines are being drawn. Soldiers from the West and from the Middle East passionately believe that their cause is just and that God is on their side. Whatever your political persuasion or viewpoint on war and terrorism, the situation evokes fear, sadness, and, perhaps, deep-seated anger.

There's something unsettling about linking images of hatred, hostility, and conquest with the concept of a loving and righteous God. We find the link unsettling enough when we think about the medieval Crusades, and we feel even more uncomfortable when we hear the connection today. It is especially disquieting to the current generation of pre-Christians who have been raised on peace protests and antiwar rhetoric. Even the language of some of our most cherished hymns sounds barbaric and bloodthirsty to their ears:

"Onward, Christian soldiers! Marching as to war,
With the cross of Jesus going on before!
Christ, the royal Master, leads against the foe;
Forward into battle, see, his banners go...

I have seen Him in the watch fires of a hundred circling camps;
They have builded Him an altar in the evening dews and damps;
I can read His righteous sentence by the dim and flaring lamps;
His day is marching on..."

The traditional language of outreach is filled with images of Christians triumphing over the ungodly. For example, we're going to *win* them to Christ. To *unsaved* ears, it sounds like we think we're the good guys and they're the bad guys. We are the winners; they are the losers. We hold *crusades* where we *strategically* target their vulnerabilities in order to *conquer* their hearts and minds. We seek to *capture* conversations and *break down* their resistance to the gospel. We *fight* to *gather* their souls to God.

When we're not doing all that, they hear us on the radio and see us on TV talking about *defending* our children against *their* music, *their* values, and *their* morality. Is it any wonder that they are resisting us?

It's time to put away the medieval picture of the church as a walled fortress inside which the true followers huddle anxiously, seeking protection from attacking pagan barbarians. Christians live inside—in the light—and all the evildoers are outside in the darkness. Occasionally the purest, bravest, and most cunning knights, who have been specially trained for the task, rally the troops and lead them out of the walls to wage a holy crusade.

> It's time to put away the medieval picture of the church as a walled fortress inside which the true followers huddle anxiously, seeking protection from attacking pagan barbarians.

When they are victorious, they return to the castle with all the captives they have liberated from the enemy. For far too long, this subliminal story has shaped our fears and inspired our evangelistic strategies.

The idea of moving away from military language is catching on even in the most conservative evangelistic circles. At The Billy Graham Evangelistic Association, people are now calling their stadium gatherings missions instead of crusades because they've realized that for many the word *crusade* elicits images of medieval soldiers murdering and plundering their way through the Holy Land on horseback. The word *mission* is a more welcoming term to the people they hope to reach with the good news of Christ.

A New Angle on the Gospel

Saint Francis of Assisi called himself God's acrobat because he frequently had to stand on his head in order to see things God's way. He saw that the beloved parables of the Lord Jesus were powerful precisely because they turned deep-rooted stereotypes about God and religion completely upside down. In the book of Matthew, Jesus "painted" many pictures—using simple images his listeners could easily follow—to show how his kingdom would be completely different from what they expected:

- a man sowing seed in his field, Matthew 13:24-30
- a tiny mustard seed, Matthew 13:31-32
- yeast added to dough, Matthew 13:33
- treasure hidden in a field, Matthew 13:44
- a net catching all kinds of fish, Matthew 13:47-50
- a king settling accounts with his servants, Matthew 18:23-35
- a landowner hiring men to work in his vineyard, Matthew 20:1-16
- a king preparing a wedding banquet for his son, Matthew 22:2-14
- bridesmaids who went out to meet a bridegroom, Matthew 25:1-13

Perhaps it's time to join Jesus and Saint Francis by standing some of our old pictures of evangelism on their heads and looking at them from some fresh, new angles. We could even paint some completely fresh pictures in terms that are familiar and yet intriguing to those we hope to touch. If stretching ourselves beyond our comfortable and familiar ways gives people new insights into the compelling character of our loving God, is it worth the effort?

When God's Spirit and his love begin communicating through us effectively, an uncontainable energy awakens in our lives, our churches, and in the world of people around us. Everybody becomes hungry for more. When we talk about evangelism being irresistible, we mean something so appetizing and so cool that no one can walk past it without becoming hungry.

God's City and Man's City

According to C.S. Lewis, "all that is not eternal is eternally out of date." Saint Augustine wrote about the same theme in his ageless classic *The City of God*. We can save you from laboring through that book of approximately a thousand pages with Steve's versions of a Cliff's Notes summary. According to Augustine, the City of God and all that comes with it will endure throughout all the ages. All that is good and true and pure comes from this eternal city. Every human being is on a quest to find this heavenly El Dorado.

Augustine's City of Man provides shoddy imitations of our heart's desires—imitations doomed to decay and obsolescence—that bring nothing but frustration. Gaining the City of Man is as disappointing as ending up with a Yugo when you wanted a Lexus. We are all looking for love, joy, peace, patience, and all the other fruit of the Spirit named in Galatians 5:22-23; but what we find in the City of Man is perpetual struggle, an unending lust for power, and a constant glorification of the human ego. Success is everything in the City of Man, and its citizens will use whatever means necessary to acquire it. Tragically, all man-made organizations and man-made approaches will eventually fail.

Scarcity and jealousy power the engines that drive the City of Man, where we always harbor a deep apprehension that we won't get enough. In the City of God, we find eternal abundance. We serve a God who is more than able to supply all we could possibly ask for or imagine (see Ephesians 3:20). In his city, God is building a fabulous kingdom for the weak, foolish, broken members of humankind. His love is changing them into the generous, joyful people they have always secretly longed to be.

In his city, God is building a fabulous kingdom for the weak, foolish, broken members of humankind.

Churches and Christian organizations are often located so close to the border between the two cities that we have one foot in the City of God and the other in the City of Man. The part that is in the City of Man is always shackled to a base concern for individual accomplishment and influence. In the City of Man, it is men and women who are the grand architects and who receive all the praise for the towering cathedrals and skyscrapers raised by their will. We look for mighty leaders who have the charm, the charisma, and the "magic touch" to get things done. Money and power accrue to the smart, strong, gifted, and good-looking.

In the City of God, God is the architect, and he raises up humble and broken people, including Moses, David, Peter, Paul, and Barnabas, to love and serve others. The kingdom of man is all about getting—getting more and more and more. The kingdom of God is all about giving—giving freely, with abandon and without expectation of receiving in return. In the City of Man, we find great disappointment, but anything that comes from the City of God is irresistible.

If God has placed "eternity in the hearts of men," as Ecclesiastes 3:11 tells us, why has the good news of Jesus become bad news to so many?

Our goal is to continually move away from the thinking and behavior of the City of Man and into the irresistible habits of God's city. It's a huge mental shift. (See chart on page 19.)

If God has placed "eternity in the hearts of men," as Ecclesiastes 3:11 tells us, why has the good news of Jesus become bad news to so many? Perhaps it's because people are looking for the City of God and all they are finding in our churches is another subdivision in the City of Man.

God has created all humankind with an insatiable desire to seek the City of God. If we are to become irresistible evangelists, we must seek first to find and live in the liberty of the City of God. We must look for openings to give to others unselfishly; to serve instead of being served; to invest time, energy, and prayer in them; and to focus on their needs. We must work for their benefit, sacrifice for them, listen to them, enjoy them, learn from them, and open our hearts to them. This sounds like a lot of work and a recipe for compassion burnout. And it would be if we weren't being loved, supported, and filled with compassion straight from God's city.

CITY OF MAN   **CITY OF GOD**

Temporary... ... ...Eternal

Corruptible... ... ...Incorruptible

Doomed to failure... ... ...Destined for success

Limited vision... ... ...Unlimited vision

Frustrating... ... ...Liberating

Self-seeking... ... ...Grace-giving

Instant gratification... ... ...In God's time

Loving conditionally... ... ...Loving unconditionally

Bigger is better... ... ...Small things done
with great love

Faster is better... ... ..."No wine before its time"

Results measured by numbers... ... ...Results measured by progress
toward God

Hero worshipping... ... ...God worshipping

Exclusive... ... ...Inclusive

Resisting change... ... ...Embracing the changing
seasons

Ruled by the powerful... ... ...The greatest is the
and intelligent   servant of all

Perception is everything... ... ...Reality is everything

THE DESIRE FOR EFFECTIVENESS

Doug has a friend he calls Lady Di who has always hungered to share Jesus with the people around her. She went through Evangelism Explosion training three times. She took Campus Crusade for Christ's training on how to share the Four Spiritual Laws. She learned the Roman Road approach and many other ways of leading people to Christ. Diana's fervent desire to reveal God's love to others even led her to serve as a missionary in Thailand. She diligently sought training and experience, but her testimony as an evangelist is a sad one: "I've had twenty-five years of evangelism experience, and it's been a total mess."

Diana said that no matter how hard she tried, she could never come to the point of asking "the big questions" required by the methods she had been taught. She said using the various soul-winning tools she'd been taught felt strained and unnatural.

I kept thinking, I don't know this person. Making a commitment to Christ is the most personal thing in the world, but all of the techniques I'd been taught seem so artificial and impersonal.

I had come to the conclusion that evangelism was not my gift because I never had much success with the any of the surefire techniques I learned. I tried hard and worked hard, but apparently some people are just gifted in this area and I wasn't one of them. I'd been taught that if you can get good numbers you're a success, and if you don't, you're a failure. It was as simple as that. If the stacks of financial-appeal letters I get all the time are any indication, my job may be to send money to support the truly gifted. It sounds as if the money I give will translate directly into souls saved. And the more I give, the more will live.

Di explained that, after trying what she had been taught for a couple of decades, "no one ever came to the Lord because I asked 'the big question.'" But people did come to the Lord because they formed genuine relationships with her. They came to know and trust her, and the "big questions" more or less asked themselves.

Lady Di and millions like her have discovered what's *resistible* about evangelism. They are staying away from sales-based techniques in unprecedented numbers. They have an inkling of what might work, though, and they are still looking for authentic ways to really connect with people. They know that most folks who don't know Christ don't hate the gospel. People *love* the idea that Jesus is for them and that he cared enough to die for them. The big problem is the manipulative way in which the message is being delivered.

Maybe you are one of those who shy away from evangelism techniques that seem to be disrespectful of people you care about because those techniques ignore who the people are. Perhaps you are hungering for genuinely attractive, exciting pictures and words directly from the City of God.

Whether you're a ministry professional, a leader in your church, or just someone who loves the Lord, you know that once again "the times they are a-changin'." Everybody can sense it. Something new is pulling on our hearts. Let's get past our fears and objections and catch the irresistible tide of God's love. Let's embrace new pictures and paradigms that will open up God's message of good news to those who are far away and those who are close by. Hold on to your seats, put on your safety helmets, buckle your seat belts—it's going to be a great ride!

Something new is pulling on our hearts. Let's get past our fears and objections and catch the irresistible tide of God's love.

ENDNOTE

1. It has come to our attention that some have assumed that the word *irresistible* in our title means that we are championing the doctrine of irresistible grace. The fact is, we are using the word in a very common, nontheological way. The idea is that most people aren't saying no to Jesus, but to the unappetizing way the church presents him. This book is about finding ways to share Christ that are ultimately so genuine and desirable that they are far more difficult (but not impossible) to resist.

Good INTENTIONS

> "I reach out in love,
>   my hands are guns,
> my good intentions
>   are completely lethal."
>   —MARGARET ATWOOD,
>   "IT IS DANGEROUS TO
>   READ NEWSPAPERS"

> "There is a way that seems
> right to a man, but in the end
> it leads to death."
>   —PROVERBS 14:12

The old saying that the road to hell is paved with good intentions is true in at least two ways. Most people use it to point out that good intentions without good actions are worthless. Used this way, the adage offers biblically sound advice; 1 John 3:18 admonishes us not to love others with pretty words, but to put our words into practical actions. It's a little kick-in-the-pants reminder to put up or shut up or, as pop psychologist and moralist Dr. Laura Schlessinger loves to say, "Now go do the right thing!"

On the other hand, what if the things we're doing with the best of intentions have "hellish" results for the people we're trying to help? What if, to borrow a line from a poem by Canadian novelist Margaret Atwood, our "good intentions are completely lethal"?

Good intentions, it seems, almost killed Elizabeth Barrett Browning, the Victorian poet. The story is told that, although she had already made a name for herself as a writer, she endured five years of unhappy captivity, shut in her bedroom in her father's house. To protect Elizabeth's "delicate constitution" from the frequent respiratory illnesses she had suffered since childhood, her father restricted her to her bed, severely limited visitors, and ordered servants to give her large medicinal doses of opium every day. Much of the time she lived in a state of near stupor, often unable to think clearly or function for herself. To make matters worse, opium addiction perpetuated a state of lingering sickness that reinforced her status as a helpless invalid.

If this sounds inhumane, remember that it happened when opium was the latest wonder drug. It was the secret ingredient in most popular patent medicines of the time. Elizabeth's family members were doing their best to provide state-of-the-art medical care. They loved Elizabeth and genuinely feared losing her. However, with the very best of intentions, they were destroying her spirit and perhaps quite literally killing her with kindness.

Our best intentions are quite literally driving people away from the Lord and even speeding their progress on the "highway to hell."

Sadly, countless Christ-loving, Bible-believing churches are making the same mistake. We might care deeply about the people who don't yet know Jesus. We might fear for their eternal souls. We may even try our best to correct and warn them. Meanwhile our best intentions are quite literally driving people away from the Lord and even speeding their progress on the "highway to hell."

Dave tells the story of how a well-intentioned preacher nearly destroyed the fruit of more than four years of prayer and evangelistic work in his early life:

I didn't know it at the time, but throughout junior high and high school a group of religious kids everybody called the God Squad was praying for me once a week. And they didn't just pray. They were constantly reaching out to me and trying to befriend me, even though I was about as different from them as I could possibly be.

In a conservative, little Midwestern town of just over seven thousand people, the sullen, long-haired, pot-smoking "stoner" Navy brat from California (who distributed Chairman Mao's little red book and scrawled, "Students of the world unite!" on all the blackboards) stood out just a little bit. Although I frequently mocked and sarcastically rejected their offers of friendship, the eight or so God Squad kids didn't seem to mind. I thought they were all a bunch of strait-laced dorks, but as the years rolled on, they kind of grew on me.

Then Chuck, a fellow stoner, began hanging around with the God Squad kids. When he asked me to go to church with him one Wednesday night, I said yes. I put on my best orange-and-purple-flowered crepe shirt (with the wide, Jackson Five collar that reached my armpits) and my purple crushed-velvet bell-bottoms, pulled my hair back in a three-foot-long ponytail, and went to church. My connection with the God Squad and with Chuck had made me curious about God. I had already been secretly reading the Bible and even praying a little. Years of God Squad work and prayer were starting to pay off. I was right on the edge of coming to Christ.

Chuck and I took seats up front by the podium. Then the preacher came forward, looked right at Chuck and me, and put aside his sermon text. He spontaneously opened his Bible and read 1 Corinthians 11:14 in thunderous King James English. "Doth not even nature itself teach you, that, if a man have long hair, it is a shame unto him?" Looking straight at me, he proceeded to lecture for thirty minutes about the evils of men wearing their hair long. Then he turned to Deuteronomy 22:5 and lectured for another thirty minutes about how men dressing in womanish clothing is an abomination to God.

I was so unfamiliar with church language and church people that I didn't understand most of what the preacher was talking about until years later. So when the preacher eventually invited anyone who wanted to pray to come forward to the altar, I only hesitated for a minute. As I knelt, an older woman in a flower-print dress gave me a strange look, scooted as far away from me as she could possibly get, and resumed her praying.

Her reaction spoke to me far louder than the hour-long sermon had. In that moment, I finally got the picture. People like me would never be welcome in this church. People there showed no interest in getting to know or care about the person I was inside.

The preacher and the people in the congregation were not bad people. They weren't trying to be mean or to alienate anyone. Their intentions were honorable. They wanted to lift up and live out the Word of God, even when what it said was not popular. Unfortunately their good intentions drove Dave away from church with a bad taste in his mouth.

Without the loving persistence of his friends from the God Squad, who kept on praying and reaching out to him, Dave's church experience could have been a spiritual disaster. As it was, several more months passed before Dave did give his heart to Jesus. It's no coincidence that a few years later he entered into his life's work of helping Christians learn to listen and communicate God's caring to people in genuinely respectful ways.

In this new millennium, it is rare to hear a sermon about sinful hairstyles, or sin itself, but pre-Christians are still coming away from encounters with us feeling wounded and disrespected.

In this new millennium, it is rare to hear a sermon about sinful hairstyles, or sin itself, but pre-Christians are still coming away from encounters with us feeling wounded and disrespected. This is especially true when it comes to evangelism.

Is it any surprise that the culture we live in dislikes and disrespects Christians? As a wise old church janitor once explained to a new pastor fresh out of seminary: "Don't you forget, boy, with people most times, you gets what you gives!" If we fear not-yet-Christians, they will be afraid of us. When we condescend to them and disrespect them, they naturally return the favor. The nearly universal disrespect of Jesus-followers in Western culture is a huge obstacle to evangelism. But where does it come from?

SEVEN DEADLY SINS OF EVANGELISM

Can you name the seven deadly sins? Do you know what is deadly about them? (No, this is not a bar bet. We're serious.)

Well, the seven deadly sins are attitudes and behaviors that thirteenth-century monks identified as particularly lethal to spiritual growth. They are pride, covetousness, lust, anger, gluttony, envy, and sloth. Did you notice that these are things we're all at risk to do? Nobody is exempt from all seven, not even such great saints as Billy Graham and Mother Teresa. OK, Mother Teresa is in heaven now, so she's beyond temptation, but everyone alive today stands in some peril of falling.

Deadly sins are sneaky and seductive. At first they don't look or feel wrong at all.

Deadly sins are sneaky and seductive. At first they don't look or feel wrong at all. C.S. Lewis was fond of pointing out that the worst sins are just "bent virtues." For example, with just a slight twist, Satan can bend courage and self-confidence into pride. He turns love to lust and admiration to envy. Since everyone is a little bit messed up, we all fall—even when we have the best intentions (see Romans 7). This is a book about evangelism, though, so the seven deadly sins we're going to talk about are the ones that contaminate and cripple our efforts to communicate Christ's good news in a way that opens hearts and changes lives.

We live in a post-Christian age. It's a confusing new environment where the rules of communication between Christians and unchurched members of our culture have changed radically. The messages and methods the church has used for decades are now misunderstood or perceived as ugly and negative by the world around us. We use words that have resonated powerfully and stirred hearts for centuries, but our culture redefines those words and reshapes the nuances in the ears of our hearers so that our words no longer mean what we intend.

In this age, we need to communicate in straightforward terms—without religious shadings or pretense. Pre-Christians can detect less-than-genuine messages from miles away. When we say, "I love you and God loves you," but then demonstrate by our actions that we really mean, "I will love you as long as you think like me, conform to my standards of behavior, and look pretty much like me," people will believe the behavioral message every time. They must see the truth clearly acted out in the Christian's life before they believe it and join up.

Several common but insensitive and ineffective evangelistic approaches are especially deadly in the current cultural context. Some of these methods might have worked at other points in the centuries of church history (Emperor Constantine's famous "convert now or we'll chop off your head" approach, for instance), but they certainly don't work now. We call these approaches deadly sins because they're often spiritually fatal and they almost always cause serious emotional and spiritual injury.

Don't be surprised if you recognize someone you know among the following characters. If you're like most of us who've come to faith in a traditional church, you may even have invested wholeheartedly in the practice of one or more of these "sins," thinking it was an approved soul-winning tool.

Deadly Sin #1—Scheming

In the average unchurched person's mind, the word *evangelist* brings up an image of a flamboyant, big-haired, oily, Bible-thumping preacher who makes his living by deceiving and swindling ignorant and gullible people. There are, in fact, more than

When we say, "I love you and God loves you," but then demonstrate by our actions that we really mean, "I will love you as long as you think like me, conform to my standards of behavior, and look pretty much like me," people will believe the behavioral message every time.

a few charlatans out there who match this description and give evangelism a bad image.

As the evangelism director for Athletes in Action, Doug has learned how negatively the average pre-Christian views evangelism.

"I really struggle with my job title," he explains. "People generally think of an evangelist as someone who manipulates people emotionally to get into their pockets. As you can imagine, this is not the kind of public-relations buzz that gets me invited to lots of parties."

What many Christians see as an unfair and annoying public-relations problem actually stems from a tragic reality. Right this minute, hundreds of well-meaning (and some not so well-meaning) church and parachurch leaders are promoting subtly dishonest schemes specifically designed to entice and fool folks into hearing the gospel and getting saved. Some schemers really are out-and-out frauds seeking to "fleece the flock" the way Steve Martin's faith-healer character did in the movie *Leap of Faith*.[1] But most schemers are sincere Christians operating with good intentions and with a passion for reaching lost people by any and all means available.

P.T. Barnum's famous line about a sucker being born every minute is the subliminal mantra of every schemer. Whether they are sincere or insincere, schemers are constantly working some sort of angle to take advantage of unsuspecting people. The classic bait-and-switch scheme of con artists and shady carnival operators is also the trademark of far too many evangelists.

Doug tells of outreach projects where students take summer "tent-making" jobs to support themselves while receiving ministry training at night and on weekends. So far, so good. This is an effective idea right out of the New Testament. The problem comes when the students are instructed to invite their daytime employers to a special "appreciation dessert." The employers are led to

> Right this minute, hundreds of well-meaning (and some not so well-meaning) church and parachurch leaders are promoting subtly dishonest schemes specifically designed to entice and fool folks into hearing the gospel and getting saved.

believe that they are coming to be specially honored, but the real focus of the evening is an evangelistic rally targeted specifically at them. Bait-and-switch.

The organizers' intentions are great, but more than a few of the comment cards from employers express irritation at being invited under false pretenses. The good will built over many weeks of relationship with their student employees is replaced with the bitter taste of deception.

Nobody likes being tricked or played for a fool, but many Christians feel pressured to use dishonest ploys like this one. Is it any wonder that so many otherwise spiritually interested people have grown distrustful of evangelism?

Like all sins, scheming is subtly addictive. At first we may feel a little uncomfortable, but eventually we won't even notice that we are deceiving and manipulating.

Popular evangelistic schemes include such approaches as Bible tracts disguised as hundred dollar bills, phony religious surveys designed to get a foot in the door for a gospel presentation, and "secular" business or marriage seminars with unadvertised altar calls. Additional schemes include various ploys that mix evangelism with fundraising or the selling of commercial products such as vitamins and long-distance phone service.

We've attached so many sneaky catches to God's free gift (see Romans 6:23),[2] that folks automatically distrust us and suspect hidden motives, tricks, and traps. That's why 1 Thessalonians 2:3[3] makes it clear that we are never to lure people into God's kingdom under false pretenses. Also, like all sins, scheming is subtly addictive. At first we may feel a little uncomfortable, but eventually we won't even notice that we are deceiving and manipulating. In fact, we may get so caught up in our scheming that we think we are normal and the rest of the world is off its rocker.

Deadly Sin #2—Scalp Hunting

Another negative image of evangelism that strikes fear into the hearts of nearly all unchurched people is the scalp hunter. The stereotypical scalp hunter is a religious zealot whose all-consuming passion is to fill a daily quota of souls for Jesus (pronounce that Jeeee *suss*-huh). The average not-yet-Christian feels trapped in the crosshairs of the scalp hunter's gospel gun—just another potential trophy to be stuffed, mounted, and added to a collection.

Christians who practice spiritual scalp hunting are usually deeply disciplined and spiritually committed people. They correctly view evangelism as something of grave eternal importance and sacrificial obedience. They want to fulfill their duty to God and to lost people, so the last thing they want is to be perceived as callous or self-centered. So where are they going wrong?

In his great book *Finding Common Ground*, Tim Downs tells a story that speaks powerfully to all of us who've been guilty of spiritual scalp hunting. Tim was involved in a campus ministry that challenged Christian students to go out and evangelize the campus.

We were all going to pair up and go out on campus to find someone with whom to "share our faith"...My roommate and I decided to team up, and we headed out to the streets of downtown Bloomington to look for an appropriate target. We spotted a solitary figure standing under a streetlight. He met all of our criteria: He was alone, he seemed to have nothing to do, and he was smaller than we were.

"Hi," I said, "my name is Tim, and this is Dave." I forgot to ask his name. "We'd like to share with you the contents of this little yellow booklet. Would that be OK with you?"

He turned and began to walk slowly away, his eyes glued to the sidewalk. He said nothing in response to our question, so we assumed his consent. I began to read.

As Tim and his roommate rapidly pursued the man down the street, reading and illustrating each point from their tract, their evangelistic prey said nothing; he just picked up his pace, his eyes never leaving the ground before him.

We arrived at his dormitory just as I finished my presentation. He was out of sidewalk, I was out of laws, and we were all out of breath. He flung open the front door, then wheeled around and looked at us for the first time... "Thank you," he said sarcastically. "You have just repeated to me everything that I had to listen to for eight years in Catholic school!" The door slammed behind him.

After several minutes of deafening silence, Tim and his room-mate began offering optimistic interpretations to rationalize away the evangelistic disaster that had just occurred. After a while, they landed on one that filled them with a sense of dignity and importance. It is the hymn of the evangelistic headhunter.

"The most important thing," I said solemnly, "is that we did what we were supposed to do. What that guy does with the message is up to him." It was no small feat—we had found a way to make a plane crash look like a scheduled part of the air show. Most important, we had convinced ourselves that we had fulfilled our duty as faithful witnesses of our Savior.[4]

Deadly Sin #3—Screaming

Another troubling picture likely to turn the stomachs of not-yet-Christians is that of the soapbox preacher shouting condemnation and insults at the passing crowd.

Steve was leaving church recently when just such a screamer accosted him on the way out:

She had long hair tied up in a bun, and she carried a family-sized Bible under her arm. She hiked up her conservative, ankle-length dress, jumped up on a table, and began to shout at me and the hundreds of other people exiting our church. Glaring at the crowd through horn-rimmed glasses and waving her Bible, she shouted, "Woe unto the whore of Babylon! This church is the whore of Babylon!"

None of what she said made the least bit of sense to most of the people walking past. The Vineyard church attracts mostly seekers who haven't figured out the Christian message yet, and as far as they were concerned, she could have been speaking Martian. It took two policemen to get her off the table and calmed down. Her comment as she left the building was, "I have made my witness."

You may be thinking, "Good! Here's an evangelistic sin I am definitely not about to commit." But before you relax and pat yourself on the back too much, stop and think. Do you ever find yourself perched on a verbal soapbox of Christian superiority? (If your answer is no, check with your spouse or a not-yet-Christian friend before congratulating yourself.) Do you subtly or not-so-subtly denigrate or ridicule the ideas or lifestyles of people with whom you disagree?

If so, welcome to the human race and to the illusion that whatever group we identify with is morally superior. We are the few, the proud, the truly righteous. We are superior because we don't drink or because we do, because we immerse or because we sprinkle, because we tithe or whatever. It is not the yelling and screaming that's the fatal offense; it's the spiritual arrogance that lies beneath it and fuels it.

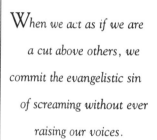

When we act as if we are a cut above others, we commit the evangelistic sin of screaming without ever raising our voices.

When we act as if we are a cut above others, we commit the evangelistic sin of screaming without ever raising our voices. Our unconscious spiritual conceit expresses itself in a stomach-turning religious pride that is the exact opposite of the refreshing spiritual poverty that Jesus spoke about (see Matthew 5:3).[5] In our experience it is not the proud and self-assured who open wide the door to the kingdom, but people who see themselves and others through the eyes of Jesus.

Deadly Sin #4—Selling Jesus As If He's a Juicer

You've probably seen those cheesy infomercials with celebrity spokespeople who team up with the inventor of some fabulous new product that's guaranteed to revolutionize your life—for just three easy payments of only $99.99. They give 101 reasons why you should phone in your credit-card number and buy their product today. Unless you're terminally bored, you probably flip right past these annoying thirty-minute sales pitches.

One of the greatest turnoffs for someone who doesn't yet know the Lord is sitting through a highly produced and stage-managed sales pitch for Jesus. Jehovah's Witnesses are trained to systematically lay out the benefits of joining their church and to answer the common objections. If you give them half a chance, they'll make an elaborate presentation. Like other salespeople, they're always looking for ways to close the deal. The problem is that most people will run, hide, pretend that they aren't home, and do whatever else it takes to avoid their presentation. Why would people treat our presentations any differently?

Steve has a good-hearted acquaintance who sees himself as a sales rep for Jesus. He has lost job after job because he annoyed customers and employers alike by sharing his faith too zealously. One of his many jobs was chauffeuring executives back and forth between their offices and the airport. In his mind, the thirty-minute drive was the perfect length of time for a step-by-step gospel presentation. Needless to say, many of his clients didn't appreciate being held captive for a high-pressure, evangelistic sales pitch. Complaints from offended customers quickly piled up and led to his dismissal and a new company policy prohibiting drivers from discussing religious topics with customers.

The temptation to treat not-yet-Christians as potential customers who need to be sold an eternal-life insurance policy is strong in our market-driven culture.

The temptation to treat not-yet-Christians as potential customers who need to be sold an eternal-life insurance policy is strong in our market-driven culture. After all, everything is sales, right? Wrong! The act of selling something carries with it a built-in assumption that the motive is profit, and our increasingly cynical consumer society has learned to distrust and avoid anything that looks or smells like a sales pitch or an infomercial.

Do you trust the TV testimonials' wondrous claims about a product that will give you washboard abs with no exercise or a paintbrush so spatter-free you can paint in a tuxedo? No? Then why should the people we talk to about Jesus accept the amazing testimony about what he can do unless they see believable results in the lives of their Christ-following neighbors and friends? A well-lived Christian life is more believable and more compelling than any sales pitch.

Deadly Sin #5—Stalking

The stalker is an over-zealous Christian who just won't leave a potential target alone. He or she is ready to pounce on any possible opening with "The Bible says..." or "At our church, we teach..." Stalkers mean well, but sometimes they're just plain creepy. Not only are they insensitive to what's really happening in a person's life, they seem unaware that their advances are unwanted. Even when people make it abundantly clear that they aren't interested, stalkers keep on talking with great enthusiasm.

Steve was so excited about the Lord when he first came into a personal relationship with Jesus that he quickly became an evangelistic stalker. He tells this story:

When I went to college in Europe for a year, I began reading the Bible and ended up coming to Christ. When I came home to the United States, I was excited beyond words. I talked to everyone about my newfound faith in Christ.

That was great. The only problem was that I couldn't believe it when I encountered someone who wasn't interested. I just pursued that person with more and more energy. The more people resisted, the more I followed them around and badgered them with provocative questions. When they tried to get away, I would invite myself along. And I wouldn't take no for an answer. I looked forward to car rides so that I could talk about Christ with everyone on board.

Pretty soon many of the people whom Steve had counted as friends started to avoid him. It was as if someone had let a shark loose in a tropical-fish tank. Suddenly all the regular fish just vanished. Steve knew they were still there somewhere, but he was left constantly circling the tank ready to pursue anyone who broke cover.

Steve had good intentions. His enthusiasm and zeal were commendable and often effective. But he was overly aggressive—his problem was that he couldn't accept the word *no*. This stalking behavior is ill-mannered at best, creepy and obnoxious at worst. In fact, our reputation for being obnoxious comes largely from stalking behavior. Nobody likes people who ignore social boundaries.

Deadly Sin #6—Sermonizing

The sermonizer is the Christian who has all the answers—even when nobody is asking any questions. This person seems to think he or she knows more than you do and is just looking for an opportunity to chime in. Sermonizers constantly lecture, argue, and correct people. Whether they realize it or not, the real agenda of sermonizers is to keep the spotlight constantly on themselves. Their motto might be: "You don't need to listen to the experts in the field, because, after all, you've got me!"

Many in the secular media delight in casting Christian leaders in the role of sermonizer. Steve explains one incident that brings this point home:

I am probably one of the few people you will ever meet who will admit to being on The Jerry Springer Show. *I was talked into appearing during its first year of production when it was a little milder than it is today. The show was originally taped in Cincinnati. I got a call asking me to give a levelheaded response to contrast the wild ideas of a pot-smoking pastor from Los Angeles. They didn't actually use the word* parental, *but I could hear that parental was what they were looking for. I reluctantly agreed to go on the show thinking that any publicity is ultimately good publicity—what mistaken thinking!*

"Pastor Bud" met me in the green room before the show. He wore a green satin cape and matching mask, and aside from the mask, he was the spitting image of Jerry Garcia of the Grateful Dead. He was a nice guy to talk to, but he had some very peculiar beliefs—that the best way to draw closer to God is by smoking pot, for example.

As we got ready to go on stage, the show's producer prompted me, saying, "Don't be afraid to get in his face and give him a piece of your mind, man!" As the show progressed, I did say a few things that ticked off Pastor Bud. And his way of dealing with the frustration was to light up a "doobie" right on the show.

During the break, the show's producer tried to egg me on by saying, "Now go in there after the break and really get that guy!" He wanted me to sermonize: to try to shame, argue, or shout Pastor Bud into compliance with traditional morality. At the very least, I could denounce his wicked ways! That's exactly the kind of no-win contest the world tries to get Christians boxed into—whether we're in the pulpit, in our neighborhoods, or on TV.

After the break, I pretty much let Pastor Bud strut around in his green cape and matching mask and silently asked God to forgive me for getting him into this mess. Unfortunately, the show was a hit on the rerun circuit, and it played four times during the next year. Friends called me from around the country to report that they had seen me on The Jerry Springer Show reruns. All I could say was, "That's just great..."

Deadly Sin #7—Spectating

Spectating is the deadliest of all the evangelistic sins. The other evangelistic mistakes we've highlighted at least stem from good intentions. But the spectator is simply afraid—afraid of the rejection that may be the result of speaking up for Jesus and afraid of failing in an attempt to share the good news. Fear of rejection and fear of failure are the excuses the vast majority of Christians use for never evangelizing.

> Fear of rejection and fear of failure are the excuses the vast majority of Christians use for never evangelizing.

Surveys by respected pollster George Barna show that 57 percent of evangelical Christians believe they have a personal responsibility to tell others about their faith,[6] but most will never talk to a friend or even a family member about Jesus. An executive from the Southern Baptist North American Mission Board recently stated that 92 percent of Southern Baptists (a denomination that consistently emphasizes soul-winning) will die without ever witnessing to another person about Jesus.[7]

The most wonderful ministry of all—the privilege of introducing people to the greatest Friend they could ever have.

Given the extremely negative reactions unchurched people often have to sincere Christians who fall into the first six deadly sins of evangelism, we can't blame spectators for being at least a little afraid. One of our goals in writing this book is to remove much of the fear and many of the excuses that hinder spectators from stepping into the most wonderful ministry of all—the privilege of introducing people to the greatest Friend they could ever have.

THE MOST ELOQUENT LETTERS

Remember Elizabeth Barrett Browning? According to the stories, her efforts to share her new life with her father are poignantly similar to the church's efforts to share the news it needs to share.

When a young admirer of Elizabeth's writing named Robert Browning was allowed to visit the Barrett household, he saw the distressing nature of Elizabeth's situation and took action. Against strong opposition from her father, Robert and Elizabeth married secretly. Then Robert carried her off to a new life in the sunshine and fresh air of Italy.

The only thing that marred Elizabeth's happiness was the broken relationship with her father, who had vowed never to talk to her again. Every day she wrote to him, expressing her love in the most eloquent terms possible. This most gifted of writers searched daily for the words to adequately describe her daughterly devotion and her desire to be reconciled with her father.

Time passed. Then, soon after Elizabeth had given birth to her first child, she received a large package addressed in her father's handwriting. She could hardly contain her excitement as she opened it. Perhaps the new grandchild had thawed her father's heart! As she opened the box, her heart fell through the floor. The package contained every letter she had sent to her father. Not one had been opened.

Today's Christians face a strikingly similar response. The best and brightest teachers of our generation have poured a huge amount of time, passion, and money into evangelism, but like Elizabeth Barrett Browning's letters, the vast majority of our evangelistic attempts are returning to us unopened.

The question we need to ask is bold and direct: *Why aren't the people we long to connect with listening to us?* That's the topic of our next chapter.

ENDNOTES

1. In this 1992 film Steve Martin plays Reverend Jonas Nightengale, a slick-as-oil flim-flam man who'll trade salvation for a donation to his touring ministry. Jonas knows how to work a crowd and a con, but his works of wonder are done with smoke and mirrors.

2. "For the wages of sin is death, but the gift of God is eternal life in Christ Jesus our Lord" (Romans 6:23).

3. "For the appeal we make does not spring from error or impure motives, nor are we trying to trick you" (1 Thessalonians 2:3).

4. Tim Downs, *Finding Common Ground: How to Communicate with Those Outside the Christian Community While We Still Can* (Chicago: Moody Press, 1999), 33-35. Used by permission. Tim's book provides an excellent examination of the challenges of communicating Christ in a changing culture.

5. "Blessed are the poor in spirit, for theirs is the kingdom of heaven" (Matthew 5:3).

6. Statistics from Barna Research Online at www.barna.org (2002).

7. Leonard Sweet, *Post-Modern Pilgrims: First Century Passion for the 21st Century World* (Nashville: Broadman & Holman, 2000), 162-163.

CHAPTER 3

Simply *Resistible* RELIGION

> "We were deceived by the
> wisdom of the serpent,
> but we are freed by the
> foolishness of God."
> —SAINT AUGUSTINE

> "And now I will show you the
> most excellent way."
> —THE APOSTLE PAUL,
> 1 CORINTHIANS 12:31B

Steve had been looking forward to it for months. He had announced it to all of his friends. He could hardly contain his excitement. After twenty-plus years of church planting, successful pastoral ministry, and traveling the world as a much-sought-after conference speaker, he was finally going to have time to fulfill a lifelong dream. In September he would be attending seminary for the first time. He tells about the experience:

I bought and studied all of the required textbooks, and when classes started in September, I was ready. The time had come to enter the spiritual and intellectual big leagues.

In the first moments of my first class, the professor (who looked and sounded disturbingly like Don Knotts) began a nasal, high-pitched lecture by explaining that any paper turned in after he opened his eyes at the conclusion of the opening prayer would receive a one-grade demerit. I was stunned!

The professor then proceeded to lecture on the connection between body piercing and homosexuality. He forbade any of his male students to wear earrings or have any other body part pierced because, according to him, body piercing is a clear admission of gay "leanings." (I don't have any "piercings," but after hearing this lecture, I was ready to run right out and get one.)

I had come to seminary hungry for opportunities to explore deep spiritual truth, but what I found as I moved from class to class was a growing list of unbelievably infantile rules. Adults were scolded and talked down to as if they were disobedient junior high school students. Even so, I could have lived with the petty rules and regulations if the approach to ministry hadn't been so startlingly irrelevant to the lives and needs of the people back home at my church.

Seminary was feeling more and more like a bad dream in which I had died and gone to church hell. My punishment was to be eternally lectured by folks who were totally out of touch with present-day life and ministry.

I couldn't help wondering how my professors would have dealt with the nearly hysterical single mother who had turned up in my office only the day before. How would the bland theological theories I was hearing sound in the ears of someone on the edge of a complete nervous breakdown? Would any of the ideas they were teaching give her more hope so she could face the overwhelming pressures of her life?

I also couldn't help wondering whether my teachers had ever actually tried the approaches they were recommending with real people or were just repeating ideas they'd heard in lectures during their own seminary days back in 1965 or so. As the day wore on, my disappointment and cynicism only increased. Maybe you've heard this uncharitable adage: Those who can, do. Those who can't, teach. Those who can do neither, lecture. Seminary was feeling more and more like a bad dream in which I had died and gone to church hell. My punishment was to be eternally lectured by folks who were totally out of touch with present-day life and ministry.

Steve drove away from school that day realizing that he would never return. He lasted a total of one day in seminary. It broke his heart to think about the irrelevance and ineffectiveness that so many earnest, well-meaning professors were unleashing into the minds of our future spiritual leaders and the lives of their congregations. For him, continuing to attend would have been not only bad for his blood pressure but an utter waste of time.

I wish we could say that Steve's experience in seminary was unique, that the problem was with just one school, or that Steve just needs better medication. But Steve reports on what he's heard from others:

Since my brief experience in seminary, many students and recent seminary grads from around the country have spoken to me after conferences to share similar experiences. A recent divinity student confided that he had just completed two grueling years of Greek study. When he asked the professor how much use he would get out of all of his study in the long run of ministry, the professor answered, "Practically none. You really need many years of Greek to master it."

"Then why do we take just enough to feel frustrated?" he asked.

The professor placidly replied, "It's part of your initiation into the ministry. Everybody has to do it."

Among the people I've talked to, the consensus seems to be that there is nothing wrong with seminary except that the wrong people are teaching the wrong things to the wrong students in the wrong way. Beyond that, it's a pretty good arrangement.

The intent here is not to critique the effectiveness of the seminary system. (That would be a very different kind of book.) Instead, our goal is to draw a parallel between Steve's unpleasant experience in seminary and what happens when ordinary people who are not yet Christians turn to the church seeking spiritual answers. Any natural appetite for spiritual insights that people might bring into their conversations with Christians is quickly ruined by an amazingly unappetizing array of "churchy" regulations, expectations, and religious traditions. Pre-Christians' experiences with churches are often tainted by a pervasive atmosphere of judgment and condescension, and what pre-Christians hear preached often seems naively out of touch with their lives and their core values.

THE WORD ON THE STREET

The word is out that our talk of love and acceptance is at best conditional. Here's the message people pick up: If you don't smoke, don't drink, don't have tattoos or pierced body parts, and don't use certain curse words, you might be welcome. As long as you're not sleeping with a boyfriend or smoking dope, as long as you're not homosexual or a Democrat, and as long you don't mind singing eighteenth-century hymns and following all the church rules, you *may* be a candidate for acceptance. Our subliminal entrance requirements proclaim that only the "culturally righteous" are welcomed and that any "culturally naughty" need not apply.

Entrance requirements fly in the face of Christ's words in Luke 5:32. Jesus didn't come "to call the righteous, but sinners to repentance." Come to think of it, the squeaky-clean religious leaders of *that* day were totally scandalized by Jesus' openhearted manner and by the questionable company he kept. Like Steve's antipiercing professor, we can be so afraid of falling into worldly traps or getting sucked into sin that we never connect with the people Jesus came to save.

Awhile back we sent a video crew out on the streets of downtown Cincinnati to ask a wide sampling of passersby what they thought of Christians. Cincinnati is a conservative city, so you might expect to hear at least a few favorable reports. That's not what happened. Following are examples of their candid comments:

"It seems like they don't care about me or my views. They're all about what they want to pull me into...They try to open me up to their 'new views,' but it's kind of like it doesn't matter what I tell them."

"It's a turn off! It makes you not want to believe in what they believe in."

"They're too aggressive. They push their beliefs on you because they want you to believe what they believe."

"I just want to get away from them."

"I'd say 75 percent of these people don't really care who I am. They just want to build up their church or something. They don't even ask me what my name is..."

It sure doesn't sound like Christ's love is getting through. These comments just underscore the bad news about evangelism that researchers such as George Gallup Jr. and George Barna have been reporting for years. In Gallup's estimation, "believers in Christian faith have some bridge-building to do in the new century; too often the message of religious people has seemed only judgmental and less than inviting or redemptive...believers need greater sensitivity than ever before."[1]

Likewise, Barna says, "Regardless of its true character and intent, the Christian community is not known for love, nor for a life-transforming faith... Outdated means of outreach, inappropriate assumptions about people's faith, and a lack of passion for helping non-believers to receive God's love and acceptance are hindering the Church from fulfilling its mandate."[2] According to Barna's research, Americans over the age of eighteen have only a 6 percent probability of accepting Christ as their Savior![3] That means 94 percent of adults who are not already Christians are unlikely to respond to Christ's gospel as it is currently being presented.

Both researchers agree that today's pre-Christian people *are* seeking spiritual answers to life's problems. However, they will rarely respond to the evangelistic slogans, guilt induction, or inept and disrespectful quick fixes typically offered by well-meaning believers. Gallup points to ineffective outreach as a major cause of declining church attendance. "The loss of church members in most

> In Gallup's estimation, "believers in Christian faith have some bridge-building to do in the new century; too often the message of religious people has seemed only judgmental and less than inviting or redemptive...believers need greater sensitivity than ever before."

Christian denominations in recent decades can be traced in part to a lack of intentional (and informed) evangelism."[4]

In the year 2000, roughly half of all churches in America did not add one new person through conversion! Churches in Canada and Western Europe are faring the same.[5] But lack of conversion is not due to a lack of conviction about the need for evangelism. Most Christians believe strongly that evangelism to adults is important. While the gospel message receives vast exposure on radio and TV, in churches, through mission groups, and through many other kinds of outreach, the message is falling on increasingly deaf ears in today's world.

The message is falling on increasingly deaf ears in today's world.

Steve's negative seminary experiences line up pretty closely with the dreary reports we're hearing about the church's attempts to reach out evangelistically. Statistics for the year 2001 placed the total cost of evangelistic outreach at an average $330,000 for each and every newly baptized believer![6] Yet unwavering tradition and hefty endowments allow the system to march blindly forward without ever stopping to ponder this abysmal lack of results. All the while, we either charge ahead full force, continuing to alienate the very people we are trying to reach, or settle drowsily into our church routines without ever giving a thought to the spiritual needs of our neighbors.

So what's the antidote to these troubling trends?

IS THERE AN ANSWER?

We wrote this book because each of us fervently believes there are powerful, grace-filled solutions for all of the problems we've discussed. However, these solutions may not come easily. They require that we reshape our churches so they're no longer passive places where passive people "come and see." Instead we need active communities that equip and mobilize people to "go and be" living examples of God's kindness.

What does it mean to "go and be" a living example of God's kindness? Here's an example. It occurred just days after Steve drove away from his disappointing taste of seminary. Amazingly, it was an experience that produced precisely the kind of excitement and theological challenge he'd been looking for all along.

About a dozen of us from the Vineyard Community Church in Cincinnati packed up and went cross-country to the Black Rock Desert just north of Reno, Nevada, to minister to the twenty-five thousand attendees of the famous, weeklong Burning Man radical, free-expression arts festival. Free spirits from all over the world gather in hundreds of theme camps and celebrate personal creativity. For the most part, campers build art out of wood and then burn it at the end of the week (thus the name Burning Man).[7]

During that week, we conducted our own camp. We named our camp En Gedi, which is Hebrew for a stream of water in the desert, and gave out free bottles of water. Day in, day out, the scene was odd at best. Though we chose a biblical name, it wasn't long before other campers nicknamed us simply "water camp." We touched more than ten thousand people with the kindness of Christ. As thousands of people walked and biked past our camp wearing all sorts of wild and crazy get-ups (or nothing at all), we were set up to serve them in practical ways in the name of Christ.

As far as I know, we were the only Bible-believing Christians doing an outreach at this event. Some people asked, "Hey, are you trying to convert us to your way of thinking, or what?"

We replied, "When you bought your house, how long did you research what was available and look at houses?"

One guy said, "Six months."

We said, "Well, we're just presenting a way forward that's worth considering. We don't expect people to change their way of thinking on the spot. Change just doesn't happen that way. We're opening a conversation that we can continue next summer or by e-mail later this year."

That really made sense to these self-proclaimed pagans. In fact, that week we were unofficially voted the Camp With the Best Karma!

Reaching out to have evangelistic conversations with semi-naked neopagans was more eternally significant (and a lot more fun) than Steve's abortive seminary experience. What made it so fulfilling was connecting with so many people who normally make it a point to avoid and discount church people. These pre-Christians went away with a much more positive picture of people who believe in Jesus.

Burning Man is about as far from orthodox Christianity as anywhere on earth—and yet Steve and his team were able to lovingly and effectively represent Jesus Christ there.

Burning Man is about as far from orthodox Christianity as anywhere on earth—and yet Steve and his team were able to lovingly and effectively represent Jesus Christ there. Hearts were opened and nudged a little closer to God. Sure, giving out water is a small thing, but remember, "small things done with great love will change the world."

More Bottled Water

Besides being the evangelism director for Athletes in Action (the sports ministry of Campus Crusade for Christ), Doug is a certifiable "wild man for Jesus" who has tried just about every traditional and nontraditional soul-winning technique on six of the seven continents.[8]

Recently Doug led a team of excited new Athletes in Action staff-in-training to Antioch College in Ohio, an institution with a reputation as an *extremely liberal* liberal arts college. This is a school where the protests and free love ideals of the 1960s and 1970s are still in full swing and where at least someone is advocating almost every alternative lifestyle. It's a place where just about everyone wears Birkenstock sandals—really!

Armed with coolers full of ice-cold bottles of spring water to give away, the Athletes in Action visited this extremely liberal college determined to initiate genuine two-way conversations with students. To get the outreach going, Doug led his team around campus, boisterously shouting, "Hey, anybody want a cold one?" and handing out bottles of water. Here's the story in his words:

> *When students asked us what the catch was, we said, "There's no catch. This is just a way to show God's love."*
>
> *One young woman who heard this challenged us. "Whose God?" she shouted defiantly.*
>
> *I replied, "The God who changed my life."*
>
> *"What religion are you selling?" she asked defiantly.*
>
> *I replied, "None. I hate religion!"*
>
> *After pausing briefly to digest that statement, she continued angrily, "We can't stand people like you around here."*
>
> *"What kind is that?" I asked.*
>
> *"White, middle-class, conservative Christians from the suburbs," she responded.*
>
> *With a smile and the most nondefensive tone I could muster, I said, "But I thought this place was founded on open-mindedness and respect for all kinds of ideas."*
>
> *I had her with that line of thinking because that was indeed what the college was founded upon. She thought for a moment, smiled, and launched into a lengthy explanation of her religious ideas.*
>
> *After a two-hour conversation with lots of give and take, she admitted, "Normally I don't give Christians the time of day, but I like your approach. I like what you are doing and saying. In fact, this has been one of the most meaningful conversations I've had on this campus all year."*

Doug and his group built many bridges that day; the outreach had a positive impact on students and AIA staff trainees. However, some people might wonder, "What's the big deal? Nobody prayed to receive Christ, so did anything of real value take place?" Doug's answer is that anytime someone who is indifferent toward God or moving away from him changes direction and starts moving toward him (even slightly), it is a big success.

Too Much and Too Little

Steve heard this "so-what" question a couple years ago at a famous church in Florida. Authors and thinkers from all over America had accepted an invitation to share their thoughts on the direction evangelism should be taking, and many leaders spoke from both their hearts and their heads about the need and methods they were using.

Steve spoke about servant evangelism and about the need to combine the practical with the spiritual—meeting real needs and verbalizing the good news. He reports:

Almost as soon as I had finished, a pastor who had developed a well-known, early-1960s-era approach to leading people to Christ expressed his concerns about the servant evangelism approach. (I use this man's key concepts to lead people into relationship with Christ—they are golden!) He said, "Steve, I think there is too much serving and not enough evangelism here."

I've always thought that almost any approach to evangelism will bear fruit if you just keep at it faithfully, and I still believe that.

During the next several days while I was visiting that church, a steady stream of staff people came to me and said something like, "We need what you do. Servant evangelism attracts a crowd. Our approach can lead them to the Lord once they are attracted to Christ, but we can't get people's attention in the first place. Our pastor doesn't understand that. He's still living in the glory days of the '60s when you could strike up an evangelistic conversation with a total stranger and get somewhere. But things have changed radically over the past few decades. It would be great if you could merge what you are doing with what we are doing."

After hearing from so many staff people, Steve had to wonder if perhaps both approaches were unbalanced—too much evangelism with not enough serving and too much serving with not enough evangelism. It's our determination to find and use the right balance that eventually led to this book. We need to be open to what works. We need to be willing to trade old ways that once worked for new approaches that are in touch with our times.

We live in strange times that call for new approaches to connecting with the culture around us. As George Barna says, "We can't be effective if we continue to cling to the old ways, the old strategies, and old assumptions. We do not live in that era, and we cannot be effective if we behave in a manner only relevant to the past."[9] This doesn't mean that we throw out all the tools of the past. It means we must constantly live in and learn from what's happening in the present.

We need to be open to what works. We need to be willing to trade old ways that once worked for new approaches that are in touch with our times.

SERVANT EVANGELISM AND BEYOND

Billy Graham and his team came to Cincinnati recently to conduct a mission. A few days before the mission, Steve was invited to Dr. Graham's hotel room to meet with a couple of other pastors. He tells about the encounter:

I count it one of the great honors of my life to have spent an hour conversing with Dr. Graham. Though he has made a career of harvesting new believers, Dr. Graham made it clear that day that he places a high value on the planting and watering of seeds (see 1 Corinthians 3:6). He was curious about servant evangelism—in part because he was the recipient of a free soft drink at our World's Largest Soft-Drink Giveaway on the Saturday before his mission.[10]

He asked me, "How many touches have you made over the years since you started doing servant evangelism in Cincinnati?"

I did a quick calculation and told him, "Several million over the past sixteen years."

He said, "I'm convinced that what evangelistic harvest we see over the next several days will be connected with what you all have done over those years of planting and watering. Without planting and watering, there is no harvesting.

"Oh yes, and one more thing—no matter what, keep doing this stuff!"

Things did go well at the mission at Paul Brown Stadium during those four days in August. Some 250,000 people came and about 12,000 made first-time commitments to follow Christ.

We've seen servant evangelism bring many people to Christ. It's a great tool for accomplishing an essential part of evangelism that has been ignored for far too long. It works well in combination with lots of other popular tools, from Billy Graham's missions to Evangelism Explosion and the Alpha Course.

In terms of the spiritual gardening metaphor Paul uses in 1 Corinthians 3:6-7[11], each tool works best in a different phase of the agricultural process. Some tools are best for sowing seed, others are right for watering or tending the growing shoots, and still others are best for harvesting. We have the tools, but what we're missing is a practical, holistic guide for equipping the farmers and laborers to do the right thing at the right time. That's why we've teamed up to create this book on how to continually sow, water, tend, and harvest crop after crop of fruitful followers of Christ in today's challenging cultural context.

For decades we've been witnessing rapid change in the spiritual climate in America and the rest of the world. Environmental factors are shifting even as you read these words. On one hand, culture watchers report greater spiritual thirst than at any other time in their lives; on the other hand, our evangelistic strategies and methods are producing smaller and smaller crops of healthy, growing Christians.

If our churches hope to become more fruitful, we have to change what we're doing. We have to adjust our evangelism approaches to make use of the irresistible forces God designed into the human spirit. Instead of advocating one tool over another, we must learn to use various tools, depending on where people are in their journeys toward God and in their relationships with us.

In 1975 James Engel published what has become a classic scale showing how most people come to Christ progressively over a period of time. The people farthest away from Christ are assigned a score of minus eight, and people at the point of making a faith commitment to Jesus are at zero.[12] Engel recognized that to continually harvest healthy new crops of Christ-followers we need to sow spiritual seed, water new relationships, and tend established ones.

It's a natural, organic process. First, the seed of the gospel must be sown in people's hearts. But what does this seed look like? If the seed is just words, then billboards and radio broadcasts should get the job done. But words by themselves are useless unless people are listening and paying attention.

Real gospel seeds are personal, loving touches that ignite a longing inside a person's heart. They are acts of unselfish kindness and generosity that contain a tiny kernel of Christ's love for the person who receives them. Steve and well-known evangelism author George G. Hunter III calculate that, on average, it takes between twelve and twenty significant "gospel touches" for people to move from the beginning of the scale into genuine relationships with Christ.

> Real gospel seeds are personal, loving touches that ignite a longing inside a person's heart.

Every seed that's sown has to be watered if it's going to grow. The "water" required by spiritual seeds is the consistent care and active involvement of God and openhearted Christians. In the early watering stages, listening is the most important evangelistic skill. Listening done well makes it clear to pre-Christians that the focus is on them, not our agenda. You've probably heard it said before—people won't care about what you say until they see how much you care.

Watering becomes second nature to all good spiritual gardeners. It's not a symbolic gesture or a one-time event; it's a regular, repeated rhythm that we get into as we wait patiently for the hidden miracles of growth to take place. Gospel seeds respond naturally to consistent watering combined with the light of God's truth. Hard shells soften and open until, one day, tiny shoots of hope begin to sprout upward. Unspoken questions come into the open, and new possibilities are considered.

Tending means removing obstacles to growth. Most people have significant questions and mental hang-ups to work through on their way to faith. Tending is the process of helping people examine the beliefs that keep them from turning to Christ and moving forward spiritually. Finally, *harvesting* means helping someone take the final steps into a healthy relationship with Jesus.

In December Steve was part of a Christmas gift-wrapping outreach at a local mall. While most of the people who came to get their gifts wrapped were thankful for this gift of service, the spiritual responses varied greatly. At one point a "customer" named Pam expressed a keen interest in spiritual things. Clearly, she was well-advanced on Engel's Scale. At the end of a stirring conversation, she asked how to get to the church and what times the services were. By the time she left, there was a clear connection.

> Tending is the process of helping people examine the beliefs that keep them from turning to Christ and moving forward spiritually.

Next in line were a man and a woman carrying several presents. As Steve began to wrap the first gift, he said, "We're wrapping these presents to show God's love in a practical way." He then handed them a connection card that explained the project and had a map to the church on the back.

The couple immediately put the card down and gathered up their other presents without saying a word. As soon as their present was wrapped, they left. Their fearful response was the exact opposite of Pam's interest. Clearly they were not far along on Engel's Scale. Steve knew that trying to engage them in spiritual conversation would have driven them further away, so he did a quality gift-wrapping job, wished them a great Christmas, and sent them on their way.

Steve trusted the Holy Spirit, feeling confident that this incident would not be the only time this couple would ever encounter God's people. He realized that he had planted a good seed and that one day (soon, he hoped) an Apollos would come along and water it. When that couple is ready, God might send a Dave or a Doug to tend the seed and to bring in an ultimate harvest.

The four steps of planting, watering, tending, and harvesting are essential. Unfortunately, most Christians have only been trained for and given tools to be effective in perhaps one of these four critical stages. The major worldwide evangelistic organizations have focused mostly on harvesting without emphasizing planting, watering, or tending. The result is that their evangelistic efforts now reach only those people who are already high on Engel's Scale (which means that they are already very close to coming to Christ).

A holistic approach to evangelism—one that addresses all of the developmental stages in growth toward Christ—will produce powerful results in the lives of Christians and not-yet-Christians. When people encounter the love of God communicated powerfully and personally in a way that's appropriate to where they are in their growth process, it's simply irresistible!

Looking Into the Evangelistic Mirror

Think about your evangelistic style. Which of the following words in each column best describe the evangelistic approaches you've been taught?

Monologue... ...Dialogue

Compelling proof... ...Compelling stories

Presentations... ...Conversations

Words... ...Images

Our language... ...Their language

Us/them... ...Fellow travelers

Count conversions... ...Count conversations

Front-door approaches... ...Back-door approaches

Fishing from the bank... ...Swimming with the fish

Believe to belong... ...Belong before believing

Event driven... ...Context driven

Come and see... ...Go and be

Scripted... ...Spontaneous

Winning... ...Nudging

Gospel presentations... ...Gospel experiences

ENDNOTES

1. George Gallup Jr. and Timothy Jones, *The Next American Spirituality: Finding God in the 21st Century* (Colorado Springs: Cook Communications, 2000), 160.

2. George Barna, "Barna Identifies Seven Paradoxes Regarding America's Faith," Barna Research Online (December 17, 2002), www.barna.org.

3. George Barna, "Evanglism: Probability of Accepting Christ, Segmented by Age," Barna Research Online, wwww.barna.org.

4. Gallup and Jones, *The Next American Spirituality*, 161.

5. Tom Clegg and Warren Bird, *Lost in America* (Loveland, CO: Group Publishing, 2001) 27-28.

6. David B. Barrett et al., *World Christian Trends: AD 30–AD 2200. Interpreting the Annual Christian Megacensus.* (Pasadena: William Carey Library, 2001), 20.

7. For a closer view of this festival, check out the www.burningman.com Web site. We don't endorse all of the images on that site, but you get an idea of the pagan theme that runs through this event.

8. Those who know him are certain that it is only a matter of time before Doug comes up with a "Here's Life Antarctica" campaign.

9. George Barna, *Evangelism That Works* (Ventura, CA: Regal Books, 1995).

10. That day we touched approximately 350,000 people in a couple of hours. We also involved some 300 churches from the greater Cincinnati area—a feat that was perhaps more exciting than the actual outreach.

11. "I planted the seed, Apollos watered it, but God made it grow. So neither he who plants nor he who waters is anything, but only God, who makes things grow" (1 Corinthians 3:6-7).

12. James F. Engel, *What's Gone Wrong With the Harvest* (Grand Rapids: Zondervan Press, 1975), 45. Many modifications have been suggested to this classic scale, but it still provides a helpful way of thinking about progress toward God.

CHAPTER 4

Becoming *the* MESSAGE

"The medium is the
message."
—MARSHALL MCLUHAN

"The Word became flesh and made
his dwelling among us."
—JOHN 1:14

During the forty years since it came out, uncounted millions have enjoyed Frank Capra's holiday classic, *It's a Wonderful Life.* It remains one of the most popular movies of all time. Maybe that's because most of us can easily identify with the struggles of the film's quietly heroic central character, George Bailey.

George is an ordinary guy who dreams of building great things, changing lives, and making a real mark on the world. If you've seen the movie, you know that the circumstances of George's life and his choices to help others in need consistently frustrate his dreams of glory. One Christmas Eve, a crisis too big for even George to fix comes crashing into his peaceful life, and at the moment of his deepest despair, ordinary George Bailey is touched by an angel.

In answer to the prayers of friends and family, heaven sends an awkward apprentice angel named Clarence to be George's messenger of hope and redemption. No matter how many times one has seen the movie, it never ceases to touch the heart. Maybe that's because from time to time we all need a heavenly messenger to remind us of what's important. We need a personal Clarence to come along and remove the scales from our eyes.

So what does *It's a Wonderful Life* have to do with evangelism? Besides being one our very favorite movies (Steve's and Dave's especially), it touches on a profound biblical truth. The English word *evangelism* is a combination of *eu*, the New Testament Greek word for "good" (as in *eu*phoria) and *aggelos* (as in Los Angeles), the biblical word that is most often translated "angel" or "messenger." It sounds a little wild, but the literal meaning of *evangelism* is being a "good angel." You don't have to be a supernatural being with a halo or wings. Technically anyone God sends to communicate his purposes is an *aggelos,* or angel.

True evangelism is not merely proclaiming a message of good news; it is becoming a living representative of God's heart toward people.

In *It's a Wonderful Life*, Clarence was a "good" angel, not because of his great wisdom or his supernatural powers, but precisely because his actions opened George Bailey's eyes and ears to receive God's message of hope. Similarly, followers of Christ have been entrusted to bring God's message of reconciliation (see 2 Corinthians 5:19) to the people around them. Like Clarence, we are given the job of translating God's message in such a way that it *comes alive* for people and connects with their life circumstances.

Just hearing words is rarely sufficient. True evangelism is not merely *proclaiming* a message of good news; it is *becoming* a living representative of God's heart toward people.

While most pastors shy away from talk of angels, the people in the pews and the not-yet-Christians on the street are not only interested but often fascinated with them. The topic doesn't scare Steve because he believes an angel touched him personally while he was in the hospital recovering from a near-fatal medical emergency:

A few years ago I went into the hospital to have my gall-bladder removed. The procedure was supposed to take about forty-five minutes. It was to be a simple in-and-out affair. Not long after the surgery commenced, however, something went horribly wrong. The surgeon somehow pierced my aorta in two places with a surgical instrument.

My blood pressure immediately plummeted to a mere fifty-over-thirty and stayed there for an hour and a half. The effects of such severe low blood pressure for such an extended time are similar to those of a catastrophic stroke. Somehow I survived, but my life hung in the balance for a couple of weeks as I was rolled into and out of multiple surgeries to correct the original mistake.

My recovery experience was one long nightmare, and I have to admit that I wasn't a very good patient early on. But that all changed one night in the horribly uncomfortable environment of the intensive care unit. My doctors had me in a four-point restraint to keep me from pulling out the ventilation tube that was jammed down my throat, and for some unexplainable reason, the pain medication caused me to stay awake for days on end.

As I lay awake one night, an unusual new nurse showed up in my room. Then for several days running, she came by at precisely 2:30 a.m. She was quite stern with me and yet strangely encouraging. Each time she came in, she'd look me in the eye and say, "Relax, Steve, and give in to the process of healing. God is at work here. You'll get better sooner if you'll just give him a chance to work." The nurse was an African-American woman wearing a multicolored sweater. Her hair was done in short dreadlocks. She looked a lot like pop singer Tracy Chapman.

When I recovered a bit more and my respirator tube was removed so I could speak, I asked to talk to the kind nurse with the multicolored sweater who had looked after me during the night shift. I was told by several of the staff that no African American was on duty at that hour. And, I was told, it was strictly against hospital policy to wear any clothing, such as a sweater, other than nurses' uniforms.

Whether Steve's angel was of the supernatural variety or not, she spoke and fleshed out the words he needed to hear just then. When Steve had nearly given up and given in to darkness and despair, she gave him a message of encouragement that helped him *choose life*. That's what good angels and good evangelists do. It's something that every Christian can do; no wings or halos are required.

One of Dave's good friends, Michael Toy, a retired computer programmer who helped launch the Netscape Navigator Internet browser, is fond of saying that everything a Christian needs to know about evangelism can be learned by watching the TV show *Touched by an Angel*. What fictional angels Tess, Monica, and Andrew do in each episode is just what we Christians need to do each day of our lives.

The episodes all follow the same pattern. The angels show up and befriend people in the midst of their everyday struggles and hardships. In the guise of ordinary office workers, postal employees, or new neighbors, the three angels demonstrate genuine caring to the people God has sent them to serve. Then, once they have established a genuine relational connection, one of the angels begins to glow with a golden, heavenly light and says something like, "I am an angel, and I've been sent by God to tell you that he loves you. No matter how hopeless your situation seems, he is with you."

We are the messengers God is sending into the lives of our friends and family members, our neighbors and our coworkers.

That's exactly what we're to do. We are each called to be an "angel." We are the messengers God is sending into the lives of our friends and family members, our neighbors and our coworkers. We may feel a bit inadequate; we may feel less like the angel Gabriel and more like the bumbling Clarence of *It's a Wonderful Life*. Nonetheless, Jesus blesses each of us, saying, "Peace be with you! As the Father has sent me, I am sending you" (John 20:21). Although we won't usually glow with a golden light from heaven, our job is still to remind ourselves and everyone around us to trust God's love and mercy.

One of the reasons we like *Touched by an Angel* is that the angels appear in all kinds of places you wouldn't normally expect to find them. Good messengers—angels—meet you right where you are. In more than one episode, Monica shows up at a bar to bring God's message to someone in need. She doesn't feel any shame about going to the bar because she is an innocent being. She is free of addictions and the shaming voices that would keep her from mingling with bar folk. She loves them without fear, reservation, or conditions.

But wouldn't going into a bar compromise our witness? Aren't we called to be "Christ's ambassadors" (2 Corinthians 5:20), acting just as if God were making his appeal through us? These are good questions, and their answers have much to do with our individual strengths and weaknesses. As was discussed in the first century controversy about eating meat offered to idols (1 Corinthians 8), many genuinely loving outreach efforts by individual Christians may have unintended negative side effects on weaker Christians. Having said this, perhaps it is also worth mentioning that the weak-brother argument is a lousy excuse for handing over huge chunks of territory to the enemy as "Christian-Free Zones" where he can have his way without interference. Either way, souls are at risk.

A pastor friend of Steve's is a good example of someone who doesn't want to give up the Christian-free zones. He went to a reggae concert in his hometown of Chattanooga, Tennessee, one Saturday night to hear a guy from his church play in one of the bands. He wouldn't normally have been at an event like that, but he felt that the Lord was calling him to go and encourage this young man. During intermission, the pastor went to the concession stand to pick up a soft drink. While he was standing in line, he believed the Lord was trying to convey something important to him. A clear-cut thought came into his mind: "Pay for a beer for the next dozen reggae fans who come up to order one. Tell

The weak-brother argument is a lousy excuse for handing over huge chunks of territory to the enemy as "Christian-Free Zones."

them you are simply showing them God's love in a practical way, and then give them your business card."

As you might imagine, Steve's pastor friend felt more than a little odd about this idea. It went completely against his training and upbringing. But the longer he stood there, the more convinced he became that God was actually speaking to him. Who ever heard of such a thing—giving out free beer in the name of Jesus? Steve's friend decided that if it was sin then, in the words of the most famous of all Christian beer drinkers, Martin Luther, he would "sin boldly, but believe and rejoice in Christ even more boldly."

The concertgoers responded to the offer with good-humored surprise and natural curiosity. Remarkably, the majority of this "brew crew" showed up in church the next day. They had decided that any pastor cool enough to listen to reggae music and nice enough to buy them a beer is a man of God worth listening to.

No doubt this story will offend some of our readers, and we would not recommend this outreach approach to everyone. But giving out free beer in moderation produced some great results in this case. Why? Perhaps because this pastor was willing to risk the displeasure of his congregation. Maybe it was because he zapped a number of age-old stereotypes about the church's lack of joy and Christians being sourpusses who are afraid of having fun.

Critics who automatically denounce that alcohol-distributing pastor's actions might do well to ask if we're more concerned about our revulsion for beer than we are about loving people. Whether we drink or abstain, are we guilty of being a bunch of pious old poops? Once we become Christians, do we lose our ability to boisterously enjoy the pleasures of life? If so, should we be surprised at the way our lifestyles repel not-yet-Christians? To these reggae fans, a few brewskis (one apiece, mind you: all things in moderation) were a powerful symbol. The fans found it easy to respond to the boldness and the friendliness of the gesture.

In the South especially, but in many other parts of the United States as well, a strong cultural divide separates "church people" and everyone else. Clear, bold, black-and-white lines of demarcation indicate who's determined to be in and who's determined to be out of God's favor. This story about alcohol and reggae music probably scares some people because it obscures the clarity of those lines. Assuming you're not someone who suffers with addiction problems that rule out touching even a drop of alcohol, moderate drinking is probably more of a cultural prohibition than a true spiritual indicator.

Jesus did things that made some people crazy, especially the pharisaical "line-watchers" of his day. No doubt you know and perhaps even fear a few of these folks. They draw or call attention to a clear line, and then they build their lives on condemning those who cross over it. They themselves often come right up to the line, and perhaps even put their big toe over it, but as long as they don't fully cross the line (or get caught doing it), they're numbered among the righteous. These are the spiritual descendants of the people who condemned Jesus for consorting with sinners and tax collectors (see Matthew 9:11).

Fear of religious inquisitors like the ones that Jesus himself relentlessly denounced is one of the greatest barriers preventing Christ's message from reaching and freeing the prisoners he came to save. Our fear of judgment by others and a natural instinct for religious self-preservation constantly tempt us to violate the spirit of God's law while clinging to its letter. If we surrender to these pressures, we further alienate and drive away the drinkers, the promiscuous, the addicted, the divorced, the wounded, and all of the other sinners like ourselves whom God has appointed us to reach. This is not the route that God calls his good messengers to follow.

Our fear of judgment by others and a natural instinct for religious self-preservation constantly tempt us to violate the spirit of God's law while clinging to its letter.

As evangelistic results in the United States and throughout the Western world reach all-time lows, perhaps it is time to ask whether the problem is the message or the messengers.

Popular interest in biblical themes has never been higher. Polls consistently show that nearly 90 percent of the people in the United States believe in God.[1] Two-thirds of these people say they've prayed in the last twenty-four hours![2] Some of the highest sales figures for magazines such as Time, Newsweek, and US News and World Report are recorded for the Christmas and Easter issues featuring cover stories about Jesus Christ.[3] Although there are many renderings of his historical motivations and personality, Jesus is universally characterized as both wise and good.

The problem is not the message, but our failure to communicate it in a way that reaches the hearts and consciences of its intended recipients.

If the most popular books on the shelves of your local bookstores are any indication, people are very interested in spirituality. Each year, books about the afterlife, angels, demons, heaven, and hell are regularly among the best sellers. On the Internet, spiritual sites receive hits more frequently than sites with any other nonpornographic subject matter. Biblical topics that most churches teach about, such as helping the poor, building community, and loving others, are more popular now than ever before.

Given all of this interest in spirituality, why are people not checking out our churches? People have never been *less* interested in the church or in organized religion. The concept of salvation, as we traditionally present it, is not even something an average not-yet-Christian wonders or worries about. Unchurched people are very interested in much of the content of the Christian faith, but not in the way we present it. The problem is not the message, but our failure to communicate it in a way that reaches the hearts and consciences of its intended recipients.

In postal terms, far too many of our messages are stacking up in the dead-letter office. In the language of the World Wide Web, the worthy intentions of our messages are "bouncing back" to us without ever being received. If those we are trying to reach consistently fail to take delivery of the free gift we bring, perhaps we need to become better messengers.

How can we tell if we're poor messengers or good ones? As comedian Jeff Foxworthy might say: *"You might be a poor messenger if..."*

- your church regularly receives bomb threats after you've been out witnessing.
- your mother won't return your phone calls since she received your most recent evangelistic Christmas letter.
- your church's insurance carrier refuses to cover you because of lawsuits stemming from a "highly creative" outreach event.
- your neighbors are circulating a petition to have you remove your turn-or-burn lawn display.
- you are cited for causing repeated car accidents as people strain to read the thirty-seven evangelistic bumper stickers attached to your vehicle.

OK. So it's not time to quit our ministry jobs and try the comedy circuit, but seriously...

You might be a poor messenger if...

- you rarely or never attempt to help others find faith in Christ.
- you breathe a sigh of relief when talk of personal evangelism is over.
- the more you witness, the more weary and unmotivated you become.
- your divine appointments are becoming fewer and further between.
- you don't want to train others in your evangelistic approach because you don't want to set them up for disappointment.
- you are seeing less and less fruit despite ongoing faithfulness in the work of evangelism.

In Chapter 2 we described the seven deadly sins of evangelism. Once we've identified what not to do, the next question is, How can we become (and train others to become) messengers who not only get heard but see the fruit and positive results that God desires? Colossians 4:5 gives us answers: We are instructed to make the most of our chances to tell others the good news and to be wise in all of our contacts with others.

Finding a Person's Spiritual Address

It may seem obvious, but even a great messenger can deliver mail only if he or she has an address that clearly identifies where the intended recipient lives. So the challenge that precedes all effective evangelism is identifying the "spiritual addresses" of the people we want to reach.

Traditional evangelistic approaches tend to send the same message to every "unsaved" address; we've shown little concern for precision. The goal has been to get a general idea of how "non-Christians" think and then to prepare a generic message to which we hope a majority of them are likely to respond. In essence, we are sending all of them form letters addressed "Unsaved Resident."

When you sort your mail, what do you usually do with the pieces addressed to Resident? That's right. You toss them in the trash! It's pretty obvious that whoever is sending these messages doesn't really know who you are or care about you as an individual. To the sender, you are just one potential customer among thousands or even millions within a particular set of marketing demographics.

Every human being on planet Earth has a unique address in relationship to the kingdom of God. Some are very close; others are much further from faith in Christ. In passages such as Mark 12:34 and Matthew15:8, Jesus refers to people's spiritual addresses, saying that someone is "not far" from the kingdom or that others' "hearts are far from me."

The concept of a spiritual address is crucial to all of us who want Christ's messages to reach and change people's hearts. Why? Because messages that are brilliantly effective for those close to faith will quite often alienate and repel those who are far from it. In evangelism, as in most things, one size does not fit all.

People who automatically reject traditional gospel presentations are quite often open to the servant evangelism approaches mentioned earlier. Others who are apathetic or uninterested in

God and church are frequently receptive to relational connections with genuinely friendly Christians. Those who are curious and willing to check out the claims of Christ tend to respond more favorably to honest dialogue. And finally, people who are actively seeking and asking how they can become Christians usually respond well to simple how-to presentations.

The messages that are likely to get through to a person's heart are the messages addressed to that person's individual needs. Everyone has his or her own set of needs, but the way we protect the vulnerability we feel as a result of the needs is roughly the same. The deeper a need is, the more threatening it is to allow others access to it. The closer needs are to our hearts, the more closely we tend to guard them. That's why it's much easier for most people to talk about being hungry than to admit to being depressed or lonely. It's even more difficult to admit to being confused or frightened by the direction that life is taking you.

The chart on this page pictures spiritual needs in the center

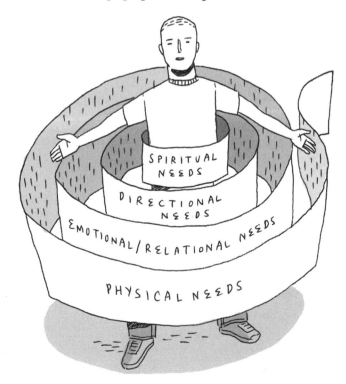

because this is the deepest and most easily threatened area of all. This is one reason most people will not trust Bible tracts or TV shows to give them spiritual help. They're looking for someone who is safe and patient enough to really talk to.

People have two sets of choices to make when considering any message. We usually choose so quickly that we're completely unaware of what's taking place. First, we subconsciously evaluate whether what's being communicated connects to any of our basic needs. If it doesn't, we will usually choose *to turn away* and ignore it. If it does connect, we'll begin *to turn toward* it and give it more attention. Once we begin turning toward the message and have started to understand it somewhat, the second set of choices kicks in. Based on a largely intuitive appraisal of the potential threats involved, we'll choose either to begin *to embrace* or *to reject* the message.[4] The more threatened we feel, the more likely we are to reject it.

Instead of making risky, direct attacks on pre-Christian hearts and trying to take them by jackhammer force, it is better and faster to take the path of low risk and high grace.

The more danger we perceive, the more violent our rejection will probably be. This is why high-pressure, turn-or-burn evangelistic tactics so often produce explosively unpleasant responses. On the other hand, the safer and more relaxed people feel with the message and the messenger, the more likely they will be to respond positively. Trust is progressive and takes time to establish. Only fools and emotionally unhealthy people allow unlimited access to the vulnerable areas of their deep heart to any but the most trustworthy.

Instead of making risky, direct attacks on pre-Christian hearts and trying to take them by jackhammer force, it is better *and faster* to take the path of low risk and high grace. Like a well-designed road to the top of a mountain, this path spirals smoothly upward and inward. If we want to be good spiritual messengers, we must learn to progressively meet people's needs in this safe and respectful order. Our most important task is to represent Christ by finding lots and lots of little ways to connect with people's physical,

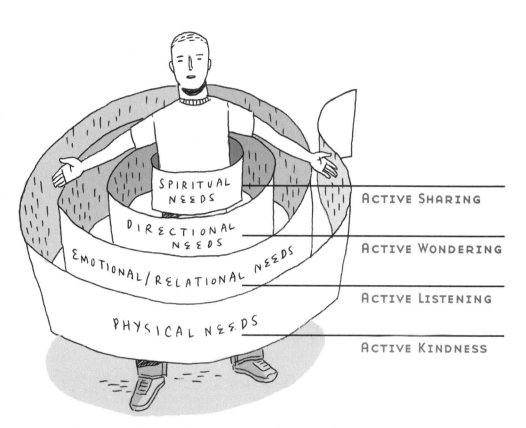

emotional/relational, directional, and spiritual needs. Forget the grand gestures, impersonal presentations, and once-in-a-lifetime events, and proceed lovingly with many caring touches that lead toward the heart.

The chart on this page shows the four basic skill sets that aspiring gospel messengers must master. They are active competencies we must make a part of our everyday lives. The first is to meet physical needs creatively and consistently. To do so, we must learn the skills of *active kindness*. We will examine these skills in detail in Chapter 6. Second, to better meet emotional and relational needs, we must brush up on the *active listening* skills covered in Chapter 7. Third, we need to put our imaginations to work on some exciting techniques called *active wondering*, explained in Chapter 8. The crowning messaging skill, covered in Chapter 9, is *active sharing*.

City, State, ZIP

Think of these skill sets in terms of a written address. We are starting at the bottom, with the state where a person lives. Then we move progressively inward to the city, the street, and last of all to the most personal part of the address, the person's name.

The trick of delivering God's mail to a person's spiritual address is really no trick at all; it's mostly a matter of caring enough to treat people with the kindness and respect we desire for ourselves. If you keep in mind the Apostle James' advice to be "quick to listen and slow to speak" (James 1:19), you will see doors open. It takes much less time than you might think for folks to allow you to connect with where they are spiritually. Problems don't usually arise unless you misread their addresses or begin pressing an agenda.

Take a Deep Breath and Just Do It!

The central theme of this book and of *It's a Wonderful Life* is that our lives, as ordinary and mundane as they may seem, can have a *wonderful* and eternal influence on the lives of others. This is good news to all of us who get frustrated and wonder if our faith makes any real difference. Dave recently received an e-mail from Brad, the son of a former colleague who taught high school with Dave over twenty years ago. Dave tells why Brad made contact:

He tracked me down after all these years just to let me know that little kindnesses, like offering him rides to school, listening to him talk about his interest in Scottish music, and openly conversing with him about my faith in Jesus, had a real impact on his life. I was shocked to learn that both he and a friend of his who is now a pastor had made faith commitments to Christ in part because of seemingly insignificant things I did.

Seeing a picture of Brad with his beautiful Christian wife and children is the best Christmas gift God could give me. I would have never guessed that anything I did years before could have made an eternal difference for anyone.

The angel Clarence in *It's a Wonderful Life* is amazingly accurate when he muses: "Strange isn't it? Each man's life touches so many other lives, and when he isn't around, he leaves an awful hole, doesn't he?"

We may be tempted to withdraw into a comfortable, safe, little world of church and family. But if we give in to that temptation, we'll lose any opportunity to touch and influence the pre-Christians God has appointed us to reach. We can *leave an awful hole*—or we can get back into the wonderful, frustrating, and often scary business of being good messengers and fallible human models of God's grace and, like Clarence, be well on our way to winning our wings.

The next chapter will focus on the specific tools we need to successfully deliver God's message of hope without being annoying or obnoxious. Think how much fun it will be to have those wings!

ENDNOTES

1. According to Robert D. Putnam's demographic work *Bowling Alone: The Collapse and Revival of American Community* (New York: Simon & Schuster, 2000), "Virtually all Americans say they believe in God, and three out of four believe in immortality." The Harris Poll (February 26, 2003) "The Religious and Other Beliefs of Americans 2003" cites a figure for believers of 90 percent, and other polls show figures as high as 96 percent.

2. George Gallup Jr. and Timothy Jones, *The Next American Spirituality: Finding God in the 21st Century* (Colorado Springs: Cook Communications, 2000), 27.

3. In her article "God Help Us" in Folio Magazine, December 1, 2002, Teresa Palagano wrote, "[A]ccording [to] data from Cover Analyzer, an information network that measures single-copy sales on 300 of the top selling consumer magazines...On average, sales for magazines featuring Jesus as the primary cover subject increased by as much as 45 percent."

In an article titled "Go Figure: The Power of Jesus Shows in Magazine Sales," (Christianity Today, February, 2003), Ted Olsen reported that magazines featuring

Jesus as the primary cover subject showed a 45 percent increase in sales and those featuring the Bible as the primary cover subject showed a 51 percent increase.

4. We are beholden to the books of psychologist John M. Gottman, Ph. D., especially *The Relationship Cure*. His concept of the "emotional bid," which he calls the fundamental unit of emotional connection, seems to provide a pretty good description of the human side of the evangelistic equation. According to Gottman, all good relationships are built through a process of making and receiving successful bids. His list of possible responses to these bids consists of turning toward, turning away, or turning against. We see four possible responses to our invitations: *turning toward* and *embracing* or *turning away* and *rejecting*.

CHAPTER 5

Golfing With JESUS

> "It is almost impossible to remember how tragic the world is when one is playing golf."
>
> —ROBERT LYND

> "Then Jesus directed them to have all the people sit down in groups on the green."
>
> —MARK 6:39

O ne of the most frustrating things in books about evangelism is a common tendency to diagnose and rediagnose what isn't working without ever suggesting anything genuinely practical to do about it. We're tired of hearing the dreaded D-word (*dysfunctional*) applied to our families and marriages—and most of all our churches—without being given any real hope of fixing what's wrong.

The $64,000 question has always been, What the heck does *functional* look like, and how do we get there from here? Since incurably flawed people consistently provide fatally flawed answers, our only hope is to find someone truly functional to set us straight. As Christians, we believe that perfect someone has come—and his name is Jesus.

Jesus spent most of his time on earth demonstrating how things are supposed to be done. He used a wide variety of simple stories and parables to open up profound heavenly insights to common Middle Eastern fishermen and farmers. His teaching was packed with word pictures that connected powerfully with people who were intimate with the natural processes of sea and sky and of growing fruit and grain, spinning wool, weaving cloth, and making tents.

Jesus spent most of his time on earth demonstrating how things are supposed to be done.

Unfortunately, many customs that early followers of Jesus took for granted are nearly incomprehensible to those of us who start each day by pouring our breakfast out of a box, go to work and spend our daytime hours typing information into another kind of box, and come home to collapse exhausted in front of yet another box. Instead of feeling that we are part of the ongoing, connected processes around us, most of us live lives fragmented into a complicated series of disjointed events.

We may participate in processes, but we rarely experience the continuity of all the stages in those processes. We might eat mountains of Big Mac hamburgers without ever considering the hundreds of little steps that bring the "two all-beef patties, special sauce, lettuce, cheese, pickles, onions on a sesame-seed bun" from the farm to the neat little Styrofoam container in front of us.

When Jesus used the example of sowing seeds to teach his followers about opening people's hearts to the Word of God, they understood the analogy because of their own personal experience. From early childhood even a fisherman like Peter or a tax collector like Matthew had experienced planting seeds in the family garden. People knew the time for planting and all the tiny, methodical steps that had to be followed to nurture those seeds into healthy plants. They knew the techniques required for setting aside seed and preparing the soil for next year's garden.

Christians raised in contemporary industrialized societies are likely to grasp Christ's metaphor in a vague, academic sort of way but miss its true power. If we ever planted seeds, we probably bought them at a store. We almost certainly never worried about going hungry if our crop failed or if rats consumed next year's seeds. To us the sowing, watering, tending, and harvesting of crops evokes picturesque images of old-fashioned farming, but we don't pick up the life-and-death seriousness of what Jesus is saying.

THE NATURAL WAY

To make use of the natural processes that open hearts and draw people toward God, we need to understand how all of the organic pieces work together to help us bear "fruit that will last,"[1] which Jesus appointed us to do, season after season, year after year. But we also need to grasp the big picture, and the big picture goes far beyond most traditional ideas of evangelism. So, before we get started, it may be helpful to lay aside—temporarily at least—a few cherished words and definitions that might obscure our vision or skew our perspective.

For instance, it may be helpful to eliminate either the word *evangelism* or the word *discipleship* from our vocabularies. If *evangelism* means "drawing people closer to God through relationship with Jesus Christ," isn't its meaning pretty much the same as the meaning of *discipleship*? Aren't we really talking about the same process? Should we think of evangelism as something we "do to" outsiders? Or should we think of it in terms of its goal: to draw everyone, regardless of his or her current spiritual address, closer and closer to the Father? As we seek to move toward God, we're always seeking to bring everyone we can along with us. In this sense, evangelism becomes something we are intentionally (and unintentionally) doing *all the time* with *all the people* around us. We no longer see it as an artificial program to pull out of our hats when we meet heathen sinners. It's for all sinners, including us!

Steve says, "Evangelism is something I just continually do—with everyone in my life, all the time. I evangelize my next-door, New Age neighbor at the same time I am evangelizing my wife, who is the most godly, 'saved' person I know." We must *all* have our spiritual arms stretched wide *all* the time to gather in *all* the people who cross our path. We need to *continually* seek to nudge them toward the safety of Christ's embrace.

We could make a decent biblical case for getting rid of the word *evangelism* and adopting the word *discipleship* in its place. After all, the Great Commission does not command us to evangelize, it calls us to "go and make disciples of all nations." If we did this, we would still be encouraging everyone around us in the same direction and toward the same goal—becoming more Christlike.

We could get carried away and merge the two words into a new one—*evangelship* or *disciplism*—to describe the whole process. But the real point is that we don't need a special "evangelism mode" that we kick into now and then to "do something to" pre-Christians. Our goal is to behave with God's kindness all of the time. We must reach out with specific, practical, personal kindness, no matter who we're with, no matter what the circumstance.

> Our goal is to behave with God's kindness all of the time.

According to Doug, Campus Crusade for Christ founder Bill Bright was fond of saying, "Everyone is a candidate for something. If it's not coming to Christ for the first time, it is learning to be continually filled with the Spirit."

Once we get beyond treating the people around us as either outsiders or insiders, we can start loving with irresistible love. If we do our best to steer *all people*, no matter what their spiritual address, toward God, we may find that the people we're steering toward faith in him include people who seem to be following Christ but don't really know him.[2] Others who have felt condemned and judged unworthy are also likely to respond. God's love falls like rain on the just as well as the unjust.[3] It's not a forced, every-now-and-then kind of love; it's perpetual. It's part of our new nature, just as it's a maple tree's nature to produce roots, branches, leaves, and seeds.

Maple trees are a great example of the irresistible processes that God designed into nature. They are remarkably efficient in multiplying and growing in unusual places. They will spring up almost anywhere a seed can find a little soil, water, and sunlight. They'll grow in rain gutters on top of your house or in the cracks in your concrete patio if you let them. We're going to use a maple tree as a picture of healthy evangelism/discipleship.

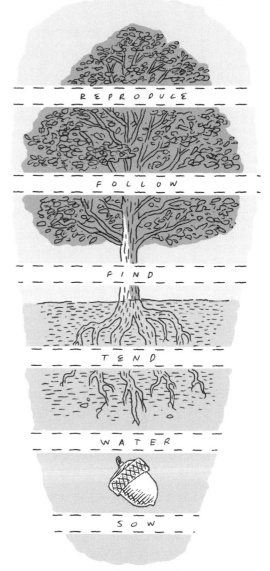

Sowing

It all starts with a seed helicoptering down from the sky and landing on the ground. A gospel seed fell into Leslie's life while she was hospitalized for depression and anxiety. Her panic attacks had become so frequent and strong that she couldn't function without heavy medication. At the hospital, she met Marge, a fellow patient, who was a former missionary and who was experiencing similar problems. Leslie loved talking to someone who really cared and who understood her struggle. Little acts of kindness soon found fertile soil in Leslie's life. She wanted more.

Watering

As their friendship grew, Leslie wondered how a person with problems as big as her own could be so open and generous. She knew it had something to do with Marge's faith, and she could tell there was more to it than religious doctrine. There was something so appealing about the honest way Marge talked—and especially about the way she listened.

When Leslie left the hospital, Marge stayed in touch and checked in with her regularly. Leslie felt a little guilty, but she really appreciated the time and attention. Soon she began wondering how she could become more like her caring, listening friend. When Marge invited her to come to a class about listening that she was helping to teach, Leslie thought, "Well, maybe I could use some help with my listening skills."

It all starts with a seed.

She attended the class and to her delight found it to be wonderfully stimulating. Since the information was centered in Scripture, Leslie grew interested in the Bible. As she plugged into the listening techniques, something inside her was ignited. She found listening to other people fulfilling and therapeutic.

Tending

At her third listening-skills class, Leslie asked her friend where she went to church, and Marge directed her to Vineyard Community Church. Leslie began to attend, sitting in the back row at first, afraid to be seen. She eventually warmed up to the point of seeking out Steve. "This Jesus stuff is starting to make a lot of sense to me," she said. "But I do have a few questions that I need to get shored up before I go any further." They talked for a while about some nagging questions, then she said, "Well, I think I'm ready to go forward with him. How do you do that?"

Finding

Steve gave her his usual prayer: "Just tell God, 'Well, here I am.' He'll hear and respond to a heartfelt prayer like that." Leslie prayed with her husband that evening. They both enthusiastically asked Jesus into their hearts. When Steve asked if they were excited, they said they felt like they were floating six inches off the ground.

For several years, Leslie and her husband, Ralph, had led separate lives. But they began reconnecting. He had always been an avid golfer, and soon she was golfing right alongside him. The only thing greater than their newfound joy of being together on the links was their enthusiasm for serving God and helping others meet Jesus.

Following

Jesus told Peter, James, and John that if they followed him they would no longer be ordinary fishermen but "fishers of men." Odd as it may sound, when Ralph and Leslie heeded that same call, they were transformed from avid golfers into "golfers of men."

Here's how they've learned to link people to Jesus: They use the tools of servant evangelism as *drivers*[4] to help people who are not interested in God move to being intrigued. They use listening skills as *long irons*[5] to help people begin to move even closer to God. They find that, when they listen well enough, asking thought-provoking questions is like using *short irons*[6] that put people who are seeking God right on the green. From there, a faith commitment to Jesus is only a *putt* away. They simply share and pray with others as Steve did with them.

Reproducing

To this day Leslie and Ralph bring a convoy of people to church practically every week. When the Vineyard Community Church holds a baptism, the people who have been involved in that person's coming to faith are invited to do the baptizing. Leslie and Ralph are always there with a long line of people they've been bringing along. This couple has probably helped bring to Christ between three hundred and four hundred people in the years since they prayed their original "Well, God, here we are" prayer.

Leslie and Ralph's "golfing for Jesus" provides another helpful picture of the processes involved in moving people closer to God. Let's look more deeply into their analogy to learn more practical do's and don'ts of "evangelistic golfing."

Using our golf analogy, picture the spiritual addresses of people who are opposed or resistant to the gospel message as on or

ON THE GREEN

APPROACHING THE GREEN

IN THE FAIRWAY

ON THE TEE BOX

near *the tee* and farthest away from the green. At this point in their spiritual journey, they have a decidedly closed or negative attitude toward traditional evangelism. It often takes many unexpected acts of generosity in Christ's name to soften their hostile stances and help them move toward a more neutral place. Servant evangelism "moves the ball" great distances by meeting simple needs with such actions as quenching a person's thirst or washing a person's car for free. No-strings-attached thoughtfulness gently counters negative perceptions and biases about Christians and Christ's message. Genuine acts of kindness work no matter where people are in relationship to God, so they are always a great way to start the ball rolling.

The second zone of spiritual interest is *the fairway*, where people are generally apathetic or uninterested in Christ. Relationship with Jesus just isn't on their radar screens. They are living their lives, raising their kids, and working at their jobs without thinking much about God. Coping with everyday struggles and pursuing emotional needs usually take their full attention. To connect with folks in this place requires genuine friendliness. Irresistible evangelists give friends practical support, meeting their emotional needs by providing a listening ear and a nonjudgmental shoulder to lean on—and perhaps cry on. As trust in a Christian friend increases, a person's openness to spiritual subjects will usually grow.

The *approach to the green* is where people become actively curious and start consciously evaluating the direction their lives are headed. Starting with a vague sense of unease or dissatisfaction, they begin to wrestle mentally with the big issues of meaning and purpose. We can help move the ball forward by asking sensitive, "active wondering" questions that stretch their thinking and open up new perspectives. If we have listened well and have prepared the way with true friendship, people will often start actively seeking God and asking lots of questions. All three of us agree that when people begin asking how-to questions they're likely ready to make a faith commitment to Christ. When the spiritual ball is on *the green*, it just takes a gentle tap. The Holy Spirit and inborn hunger for God will do the rest!

Golf is a good image because it's intentional. We start where the ball *is*, not where we would like it to be. We think about (and pray about) how best to reach the goal. Scoring, however, is often not the ultimate aim of the game. We do it for love.

Praying for the Hole in One

Steve had been playing golf for only a few months when he and a friend went out one afternoon for a round on a three-par course. Steve teed up, swung, and hit the ball with such incredible force that it flew about two feet off the ground all the way to the green. In golf lingo, this shot is known as a worm-burner. The ball hit the ground, slowly dribbled toward the hole, hit the pin, and bounced about a foot away. If the pin hadn't been there, it would have been a hole in one! The group of golfers waiting to tee off behind him began to applaud with solemn spontaneity. Not a bad shot for a rank beginner.

Of course, this kind of shot is a rarity. Many golfers play the game for decades and never hit a hole in one. It's a mystical experience that's talked about in hushed and reverent tones. Any pro golfer knows there's no point even trying to hit a hole in one because it's a chance event.

Golf and evangelism are similar in many ways. One of the big ones is a major tendency to exaggerate!

As we've already pointed out, golf and evangelism are similar in many ways. One of the big ones is a major tendency to exaggerate! We've all met leaders who have "evang-elastic" gifts. If eight people respond to Christ, the leader quickly stretches the number to sound more like eighty. The same can be true of evangelism gurus, who in their attempts to pump us up often give the impression that we can step up to the tee and hit evangelistic holes in one on a regular basis.

Most parachurch organizations and church denominations venerate a hero who was a master at making hole-in-one shots. In fact an organization's founder is often the ultimate "golf pro." People throughout the organization know "glory stories" about how the leader was able to accomplish amazing feats of evangelism against all odds. That leader could draw people to Christ right off the tee!

Within the Vineyard movement, that golf pro was John Wimber. In the parachurch group Jews for Jesus, it was Moishe

Rosen. Stories of the exploits of these men seem encouraging at first, but in the long run they actually work against ordinary people attempting evangelism. Such reports can be more discouraging than encouraging because they are so out of reach for the average follower of Christ. The hole in one may have happened once upon a time for that famous founding father—once, mind you—but it wasn't the norm even for him. And it certainly won't be the norm for you.

Perhaps it would be more encouraging to hear from the founders about the times they struggled with feelings of inferiority and shyness. Instead of spending all our time on inspirational storytelling, it might be more helpful to explain the basics in terms that even the most inexperienced duffer can use to improve his or her "game."

RIGHT CLUBS, RIGHT TIME

To understand the game of golf, you need to know what the various clubs are for and how they're used. All of them are good and necessary when used at the right time and with the proper technique. An obvious example is that you don't use the putter to tee off. As ridiculous as it sounds, this is the most common mistake that would-be evangelists make. Most of the time, it isn't their fault; they've been taught incorrectly.

As we've mentioned, when Steve first came to Christ, he was an enthusiastic fireball who wanted all of his friends to know Christ right away. He was alienating people because—in golfing terms—he had no sense of club propriety. He approached everyone with the same club—the putter. He assumed that one well-lined-up putt would bring every person to Jesus. It was an honest mistake. All of the books and literature he had read were written at a time when the majority of Americans were positioned on or near the spiritual green, so all of the evangelistic greats were masters of *putter evangelism.*

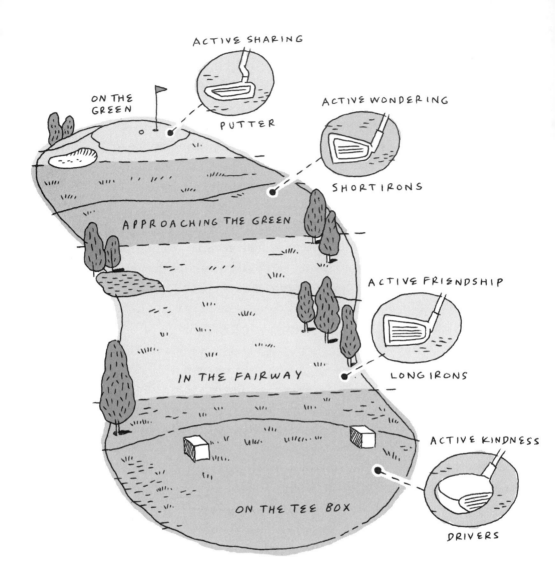

One-Club Wonders

After attending one of Dave's seminars, a wealthy business-man offered him a brand-new, two-thousand-dollar set of Ping golf clubs—arguably the best clubs made. Dave said "no thanks" to the offer. He explained, "I only know how to use one club—the putter. I play a pretty mean game of putt-putt golf, but when I try the real thing, I stink up the course. What would I ever do with such an expensive *set* of clubs?"

Many Christians share similar negative feelings about evangelism because they've embarrassed themselves by playing puttputt on the championship course of life. They were taught an evangelism approach and tried using it with their friends and relatives, and the experience was so humiliating that they don't ever want to go there again. This humiliation can be prevented if people are taught not only that there *are* other clubs, but *how* to use each one in different evangelistic situations.

PUTTER

The classic evangelistic approaches most of us are familiar with concentrate almost exclusively on the putting game—on making a convincing presentation that gets people to "pray the prayer." These methods can still be effective today if people are fairly close to making a decision. The drawback to using them is that fewer and fewer people are close enough to the green for a putter to do all the work. Using the putter with people who are not ready tends to create angry reactions and increase resistance to the gospel.

SHORT IRONS

Some evangelists have therefore become *short-iron specialists*. They are the apologists. They don't make a large group, but they get a lot of airtime in Christian circles. They tend to be the intellectuals of the church who take a more scholarly approach to convincing people to come to Christ. Using the tools of philosophy, logic, and fast-paced rhetorical exchange, they seek to promote honest dialogue with sincere skeptics and opponents of Christianity.

After the fall of the Soviet Union, a friend of Doug's was in Moscow with an evangelistic team giving out Russian-language copies of Josh McDowell's book *More Than a Carpenter*. This simple, well-reasoned case for believing in Christ was wildly popular with Muscovites who liked its analytical approach. It was almost tailor-made for people emerging from seven decades of state-instituted atheism. As a result, wherever the team went, the evangelists found large crowds of people hoping to receive copies. In just a few days, they distributed tens of thousands of books to people who would not only read them, but discuss them and pass them on to friends.

This approach works well only with people who are intellectually interested in how the claims of Christ might affect the direction of their lives. They are already approaching the green and at least somewhat willing to be convinced. However, they form a relatively small group of people. Those who are not ready for this approach tend to avoid the debate and view its practitioners as pushy and argumentative.

LONG IRONS

In the past few decades, a growing group of pastors and even some hardcore evangelists have become *long-iron specialists* because they realize the importance of friendship or lifestyle evangelism. Most of the people who come to Christ report that they did so because of a close personal friendship. Friendship obviously exerts a powerful influence.

Friendship evangelism becomes a problem if what it offers *is neither real friendship nor real evangelism.* It can easily degenerate into a marketing ploy, similar to tactics employed by Amway or Shaklee distributors. Instead of simply loving our friends for who they are, we turn them into potential clients. The not-yet-Christians of today are a lot more sensitive to our motives than most of us realize. When they detect hidden agendas in our offers of friendship, we are seen as self-serving, inauthentic recruiters.

Another big problem with friendship evangelism is that many Christians have few or no pre-Christian friends. Within a year after becoming a Christian, a person often loses contact with pre-Christian friends. One reason many friendship-based approaches prove ineffective is that the Christian subculture in which most of us live tends to become a pretty exclusive club. Too often our hearts and our relationships are "reserved for saints only."

DRIVERS

This problem leads us to the tee box and to the *driver specialists*. Showing people the kindness of Christ is very effective in nudging them toward salvation. And it's a biblical concept. Romans 2:4 tells us that the kindness of God leads to repentance. Galatians 5:22-23 tells us that being kind is a fruit of the Spirit that naturally springs up in our lives when we abide in Christ.

Servant evangelism is the living out of the gospel message. It's said that Francis of Assisi would ordain his brothers and sisters into ministry with these words: "Preach the gospel at all times; if necessary, use words." If we serve well, we will eventually need to use words to convey the complete gospel message. One friend of Steve's explains it this way: "It's kind of like show and tell in the first grade. With servant evangelism you *show* people the gospel in a profound way through the kindness of God. Then later, once their appetite is whetted, you *tell* them the details."

Using servant evangelism to connect with not-yet-Christians is a great idea, but failing to get around to the gospel message is a common mistake. The message needs to be explained so people can choose to follow Jesus. The Holy Spirit can open doors for us through our acts of kindness and generosity. It is up to us to muster the courage to walk through the doorway of opportunity once the heart has opened it.

Words can come naturally after serving someone because we're almost always responding to questions from those we're serving: "Why are you serving me?" "What do you guys believe, anyway?" "What's the Bible all about?" "What's the big deal with Jesus?" "Why do you celebrate Easter?" We've heard those questions again and again. We call them *real-life apologetics*—they're the questions people on the streets are asking. They're the questions that help people figure out if they're going to be at all interested in Jesus.

If we're to be effective at evangelism, we need to learn how to use all of the clubs in our golf bags—the drivers, the long irons, the short irons, and the putter. We can't focus on just one club. We need to work on the weaker parts of our game—after all, spiritual golf is eternal. We—and God—have a lot riding on the game. It is the desire of God's heart that we do extremely well at this game for the sake of those he loves.

ENDNOTES

1. "You did not choose me, but I chose you and appointed you to go and bear fruit—fruit that will last" (John 15:16).

2. "Many will say to me on that day, 'Lord, Lord, did we not prophesy in your name, and in your name drive out demons and perform many miracles?' Then I will tell them plainly, 'I never knew you. Away from me, you evildoers!' " (Matthew 7:22-23).

3. "But I tell you: Love your enemies and pray for those who persecute you, that you may be sons of your Father in heaven. He causes his sun to rise on the evil and the good, and sends rain on the righteous and the unrighteous" (Matthew 5:44-45).

4. For nongolfers, drivers (also called woods) are the biggest clubs in the golf bag. They usually have a long shaft; a wide, wooden head; and a deep face and are used for driving the ball long distances from the tee onto the fairway.

5. Long irons are golf clubs with solid-metal heads differentiated by low numbers. They are used for the longer shots that send the ball from the fairway closer to the green.

6. Short irons are clubs with solid-metal heads, differentiated by higher numbers. They are used for the short-distance shots on approach to the green.

Active KINDNESS

> "I love thee for a heart that's
>   kind—
> Not for the knowledge in thy
>   mind."
>
> —W.H. DAVIES,
> "SWEET STAY-AT-HOME"
>
> "But when the kindness and
> love of God our Savior
> appeared, he saved us, not
> because of righteous things
> we had done, but because of
> his mercy."
>
> —TITUS 3:4-5

In the months following Steve's near-fatal medical accident, lots of friends came to visit him in the hospital. Soon after showing up at his room, they would all make the same offer. "If there is anything I can do for you, Steve, anything at all, just say the word, and I will make it happen." They were all amazingly generous. Steve tells about it:

I had figured out that the best way to feel better when I'm physically or emotionally down is to give away whatever I don't have. If I don't have much money, I need to be more generous with the money I do have. If I don't have much time, I need to spend the little I do have in charitable ways. If I don't feel loved, the best thing I can do is to begin showing love to others.

I was at the lowest point of my life in every way—physically, emotionally, and spiritually; I desperately needed to give something away to get better. All I could think of that was available to me was—Popsicles. So whenever visitors asked if there was anything they could do for me, I didn't even let them finish the sentence.

"Have you got any pocket change?" I would ask.

If they did, I'd have them roll me in my wheelchair down the hallway to the Popsicle machine. They would spring for a lap-full of the tasty treats, and then we would go up and down the hallways looking for patients to give them to. The only guideline: Only patients not on ventilators could get a Popsicle!

I can't prove it, but I think I got better much faster by giving away all those Popsicles. It was my way of cooperating with God in my healing process. I had to get out of myself and get into principles that are much bigger than my circumstances—I got better and better as I gave away what I didn't even have in the first place.

Kindness activities you can get involved in

▼

GIVING NEWSPAPERS AWAY
(One- & two-person activity)

On Saturday mornings, people appreciate a good newspaper to enjoy with their coffee. We roll papers, attach a connection card to each, then give them away on a busy corner.

This chapter is about the evangelistic attitudes and skills required for *active kindness*. The basis of servant evangelism is that the active kindness of God changes hearts. *Active kindness* is synonymous with *servant evangelism*.

The unregenerate human heart, according to Titus 3:3-5, is "foolish, disobedient, deceived and enslaved by all kinds of passions and pleasures." Our fallen humanity yields the predictable results of "malice and envy, being hated and hating one another. But when the *kindness and love of God* our Savior appeared, he saved us, not because of righteous things we had done, but because of his mercy" (emphasis added).

The kindness of God activates profound changes in those who experience it. It's like tiny particles of pollen deposited on a flower by a humble honeybee. The particles of pollen don't look like much, but they set in motion deep and exciting transformations. Whenever we receive God's kindness or give it away, our hearts are changed and opened up a little bit more. Maybe this is what 2 Corinthians 3:18 means when it says we're "being transformed into his [Christ's] likeness with ever-increasing glory." We're becoming kind as he is kind.

GIVING SOFT DRINKS AWAY
(One- & two-person activity)

DEFINING ACTIVE KINDNESS

A practical definition of active kindness is "demonstrating God's love by offering to do humble acts of service, in Christ's name, with no strings attached." It's worth pulling this description apart and looking at the key words in order to gain a deeper understanding of it.

Demonstrating God's Love...

What do we mean by "demonstrating God's love"? In our skeptical age, it is absolutely essential to *show* God's love before we speak about it. We live in a "touchy, feely" society that says, "I need to feel and touch God's love before I can believe in it." If God's love *is* real, this request is reasonable!

This transition can be hard to accept for those of us who were raised on the idea that belief must come first and then the feelings will follow. We're much more comfortable with an evangelistic model that values logical (objective) argument more highly than personal (subjective) experience. The problem is that a growing majority of those we hope to reach do not think this way.

It may have been possible in previous generations to hold people's attention with words alone, but no more. In our increasingly media-driven culture, words are fleeting. People might remember the words you say for a few

hours, but they are likely to remember your acts of generosity for months, years, and, in many cases, the rest of their lives. People we serve may well forget our names and the names of our churches, but they will long remember the acts of kindness that we show them in the name of Jesus.

By Offering to Do...

Offering to do an act of kindness is a powerful and sometimes even profound door opener. One of Steve's favorite kindness out-

MOWING LAWNS
(One- & two-person activity)

reaches is toilet cleaning. With gloves, bucket, and brush in hand, he and one of his servant evangelism disciples approach gas station attendants and restaurant managers with a simple offer. "We're wondering if we could clean your toilets for free as a practical way to show God's love." Their jaws drop, and they are often so shocked that it takes them a full minute before they stutter an answer.

Usually they want to know more about who we are and why we're doing such an unusual outreach. Sometimes they're so freaked out that they make up excuses—"We just cleaned our toilets five minutes ago!" or "We have a policy against free toilet cleanings here." (It's hard to imagine the staff meeting that voted in that policy.) Regardless of the response, the most important thing is the offer to clean the toilet. At the end of the day, that manager is likely to go home and say to his wife, "You know, the strangest thing happened today. It was an ordinary shift except that a couple of guys came into the gas station and offered to clean our johns for free—just to show us God's love in a practical way! Weird, huh?"

That couple is likely to wonder about this experience for weeks, months, or even years until curiosity forces them to get in the car and drive to that church to see what kind of people are crazy enough to clean your toilet to show you God's love. It has happened countless times at Vineyard Community Church.

Some *Humble* Act of Service...

What constitutes a humble act of service can vary a great deal from place to place and people-group to people-group. In

Brighton, England, a few years ago, a group of approximately two hundred people—mostly young people—took up a special offering for outreach. They then split up the money and gave it to about forty groups of four to five people.

Each group brainstormed ideas for reaching out to the Brighton area. One group suggested giving away cigarettes to the homeless. The people in charge weren't very keen on that idea for a number of reasons; concern about the possibility of death from lung cancer was one reason. The young people's response was thought provoking.

"Out of the top one hundred problems homeless people have, where does smoking come in at?"

"Probably not very high—we'd give it a ninety-seven."

"Exactly. And what are the first couple of things homeless people ask you for when you meet them on the streets?"

"They ask for money, and then they ask for a cigarette."

"Exactly again. Now we're not going to absolutely corrupt these people with a carton of cigarettes. They already smoke. We're just going to give them a handful of smokes—maybe four or five. Then we're going to offer to pray for them."

The leaders were still a bit incredulous about the whole idea but reluctantly decided to flow with it.

That night, after the outreach effort, the church had an open worship time with an evangelistic flavor. Many of the homeless people who had received cigarettes showed up to express their gratefulness for the gift. A women stood up in the meeting and said, "Giving cigarettes to us—now that's what I call Christianity in action!"

One homeless man stood out in the crowd. He had brought his dog to the service, and apparently had a mental disorder—he kept speaking into the air to a nonexistent person—but that didn't stop anyone present from showing him love. Every time we sang the refrain of one song—"We lift our hands to you, Lord"—he would lift the dog's paws in the air. It was a memorable night for all!

PACKING BAGS IN SELF-SERVE GROCERY STORES
(One- & two-person activity)

We pack shopping bags in grocery stores where that service isn't provided for customers. It's a great activity for those who don't mind staying busy! If friends or couples do the service together, one person can speak to customers while the other is packing.

In Christ's Name, With No Strings Attached

Here is the most important part of the definition. Christians are notorious for requiring a tangible gain from all that we do. We're experts at asking what the bottom line is. We take good stewardship to a bad extreme.

We'll never shine brightly in the kingdom of God until we can sign up for activities that bring us no immediate, tangible, specific gain. We need to learn the lesson Jesus taught in Luke 6:35 about giving without expecting to get anything back, not even gratitude. The only reward we need is knowing that we're acting like sons of the Most High.[1] The watching world will never be genuinely interested in our message as long as we come across as self-seeking promoters of our little piece of the kingdom. However, the world hungers for generosity in Christ's name when those expressing it don't care who gets the credit.

If we don't take seriously the phrases *In Christ's name* and *with no strings attached*, we're just using a manipulative marketing strategy. And that's not what we want to do. We're bringing the kindness and grace of God's kingdom to earth. We do what we do for free. We aren't trying to get people to do anything in return. We aren't trying to get them to come to our church, although we will rejoice if they do. We aren't even doing it to persuade people to believe in Jesus, although we believe he will speak to their hearts through our actions.

We serve God and seek to get out of the Holy Spirit's way so that he can work in the hearts of the people we touch. Any stipulation we place on those we serve is only going to be a hindrance to the working of the Spirit. One reason some kindness outreaches don't bear much fruit is because the leaders didn't get the "no strings" idea. When strings are attached, God seldom blesses the effort.

A lot of churches have gotten the wrong idea about kindness outreaches: They see the acts of service we talk about as a clever way to run a new membership drive to pump up their numbers. But that won't work. It never has worked. It never will work.

FEEDING PARKING METERS

(One- & two-person activity)

Parking meters are a worrisome thing for downtown shoppers. We either put a coin in the meter or put a glued-on coin on a special connection card that explains the project—depending on the local laws.

Vineyard Community Church has turned down plenty of press coverage over the years. Even though lots of reporters thought what the church was doing was newsworthy, the leadership felt that bringing newspaper or TV coverage into the picture would make it seem as if the church was promoting itself. And the leaders are happy that they've kept it to a minimum.

In the early days of Vineyard Community Church's outreach projects, those doing the projects often directed people to other established churches in town. They simply weren't ready for outside people to come to the Vineyard yet. People would plead, "But we really want to come to *your* church!" The response was that the church wasn't firing on all eight cylinders yet and was just getting going. Church people told others to look for them in the newspapers under the church section in about a year. In the meantime, people were directed to "a really good church," perhaps Tri-County Assembly of God or College Hill Presbyterian.

Dave recently helped a small, urban congregation that is trying hard to grow. The people in the congregation gulped a bit when they saw the price tag for serving their community, but they were so excited about reaching out—actually doing something that could make a difference—that they gave money, above their normal offerings, to make up the difference.

The church gave away nearly one thousand soft-drink cans and water bottles and sponsored a neighborhood barbecue for which local companies donated all the ribs, burgers, and hot dogs.

The people had great fun, but they became a little discouraged when their efforts didn't immediately produce a huge flood of newcomers through the doorway of the church. The congregation of twenty-five added a single mom, her daughters, and occasionally her boyfriend, but some felt that wasn't much fruit for all their effort. There was no problem with the outreach or with their sowing of some fine seeds in the community. The only problem was that they were focusing on numbers, becoming impatient, and thinking about giving up sowing too soon. Seeds need time to grow. Small churches in particular must be willing to give kindness outreaches plenty of time—and maintain a more relaxed long-term perspective.

In sixteen years of experience with kindness outreaches in churches of many sizes and in several different countries, Dave is convinced that the primary reason small acts of kindness are so powerful is that they change the hearts of the givers. Every time you meet someone and show that person even the smallest picture of God's kindness, your own heart is enlarged. By acting like Jesus, you become more like him.

With that in mind, it's easy to see why serving from the wrong motivations will bring the wrong results. When people fail at servant evangelism, it's usually because of selfish motivations. Growing your church and getting media attention are inward-focused motivations. But when people serve to show God's love in practical ways, the hearts of the people in the congregation begin changing and focusing outward. People start being friendlier and more generous to coworkers and neighbors, so that those they invite to church really want to check it out. Church growth happens naturally when we seek to show kingdom kindness first.

It's tempting to overanalyze outreach efforts and to focus on wrong results. Six months will typically pass before the full fruit of servant evangelism appears in a local church. Until that time, it's best to just keep your efforts going and not look inwardly at all. In fact, it's smart to spend the better part of a year doing kindness projects before looking at how many new people have come into the church. Experience shows that your church *will* grow from doing servant evangelism. It just will. It has happened hundreds of times. Your church will begin to grow as people bring their friends to church once they realize, "Hey, this is becoming a friendly, inviting, warm place that I can bring my friends to."

When Steve first came to Cincinnati to plant the church, he took a job as a school-bus driver to make ends meet. He tells about the impact of that job.

I got up early, about 5:30 a.m., to make my first shift. One morning I was complaining to God about the lack of results I was seeing with my fledgling church plant. After talking to close to two thousand people in nearly two years of preparatory efforts, we had just thirty-seven show up for our first service! I moaned to the Lord, "Why aren't more people coming to my church, Lord? There's got to be a more lucrative way to be miserable for you."

I didn't expect God to talk back to me about my complaints, but I sensed him speaking to my heart: Why would I want to come to your church? Your church is boring! But if you will go out and serve the people that I care about—the poor, the needy, the divorced, the lonely—then you will see more people coming than you know what to do with.

In the years since this little conversation with God, the church has indeed attracted thousands of the poor, needy, divorced, and lonely. More than six thousand people now show up every weekend. They come from every background: Some are doctors and lawyers; others are unemployed and addicted. There are even a few unemployed, addicted doctors and lawyers! The one thing most of them have in common is that, before they came to Vineyard Community Church, they weren't consciously seeking God at all; he wasn't really on their radar screens. Although many call us a seeker *church, most "seekers" they are referring to only began to seek when something awakened their appetite. That something is often lots and lots of little touches of kindness.*

BIG IDEAS OF ACTIVE KINDNESS

So what's the big idea? Actually there are at least four "Aha's" you need to grasp to make kindness outreaches work in your ministry setting:

Aha #1: Make It Simple Enough for Simple People

The first thing we need to understand is that *evangelism is doable.* Anyone can pull it off without a big budget or big-time experts. We have to get over the false belief that only highly intelligent, extremely gifted people with amazing testimonies and dramatic calls from God can ever succeed in evangelism. You don't even need a first name that ends with the letter "y," like Billy, Bobby, or Jimmy. These preconceptions won't die on their own—we've got to kill them! The two biggest reasons people don't want to evangelize are fear of rejection and fear of doing it wrong.

● **THE HEAD-TO-HEAD VERSUS HEART-TO-HEART APPROACH**

Both fears stem from our old picture of evangelism as a head-to-head confrontation. We've seen the experts launch frontal attacks on the not-yet-Christian's faulty worldview. They've memorized the perfect clever answer to every possible objection to Christianity. But even the pros frequently come across sounding like an annoyed parent talking down to an ignorant and disobedient child. Maybe that approach is OK for the experts, but most ordinary Christians are thinking, *I'm not smart enough, I'm not good enough, and people won't like me.* And they are probably right.

SERVING FREE HOT DOGS

(Larger-group activity)

We set up shop at a strip mall and hand out free hot dogs and soft drinks. We use a hot dog wagon, but you can make it a lot simpler with just buns, condiments, and a kettle full of hot dogs.

Before we start preaching to pre-Christians' heads, we must encounter people at the heart level. We must demonstrate that they are important to God and perhaps vice-versa. Acts of generosity and kindness that anyone can do are a low-threat way to get this job done. Once people have begun to trust us enough to open their hearts, they're usually more than ready to open their minds to the verbal message of Christ's love.

Steve tried to win one of his sisters to Christ using the head-to-head method. He had read enough about how to get people to pray "the prayer" that he had nearly mastered the approach. When the opportunity came during a long car ride, he was all practiced up and ready for the encounter. Through much argument and bulldog persistence, he convinced her to pray a commitment to Christ. Unfortunately, her "forced conversion" wasn't deep or lasting. She showed virtually no life change until much later, after she had a heart-level encounter with Christ that really "took." Then she started living a consistent and growing Christian life.

Steve learned from his head-to-head evangelism experience and went back to the drawing board. With another sister, he tried a more heart-to-heart approach. He served his way into her life. He looked for dozens of little ways to live out his faith in her presence. He gave her rides without hesitation or complaining. He gave her money when she needed it. He was generous with compliments. In short, Steve acted like a loving brother. She took notice and quickly opened her heart to Jesus.

● THE LOW-RISK, HIGH-GRACE APPROACH

A high-risk outreach is one that's likely to meet with rejection when we step out to do it. The higher the risk, the more expert the participants need to be. Traditional evangelism abounds with high-risk ventures. Taking a fake survey at the beach becomes a high-risk confrontation at the moment the participant realizes you're really trying to evangelize him or her. Virtually everyone who's normal is likely to have a negative experience. It's like being sent to the Russian front by Colonel Klink, a bad trip that few—if any—will have any desire to repeat. The high-risk, low-grace approach is Russian-front evangelism. Everyone's afraid of going there. It's highly unlikely that the people in our churches will ever want to do evangelism if this is what they expect.

A low-risk venture is one that's unlikely to fail. Giving away bottles of cold water with connection cards is low risk. One lady recently asked Doug if he had any Evian water. He didn't—all he had was a generic, local brand—and she wasn't interested. That's

> **WASHING WINDSHIELDS AT SELF-SERVE GAS STATIONS**
> *(One- & two-person activity)*
>
> We get permission from station managers to wash windshields. For customers it's just like the good old days when the gas stations they went to were "service" stations. The key is having a good squeegee and learning how to use it without leaving streaks!

about the worst rejection you'll encounter in kindness outreach: someone wanting Evian! We don't know about you, but we can handle that sort of rejection.

By *grace* we mean our level of dependence upon God to achieve the goal. If we are high in grace, we are depending upon God for

REPAIRING AND
TUNING UP
BICYCLES

(One- & two-person activity)

the success of our outreach. Why wouldn't we always have a high-grace attitude? In some ways, it's harder to depend on the power of the Holy Spirit than on our own wisdom to bring a successful outcome. It can be more comfortable to blindly follow the steps of an often-used cookbook recipe than to depend on the Spirit's enabling. Of course, he has always been and will always be the fundamental reason for any success we may experience.

When we combine low risk with high grace, we have something the average person—even the average child—in your church can do. We focus on activities that won't scare people away after an outing or two. Peter Wagner notes in his research that only about 10 percent of the general church population is attracted to evangelism. We look for things the other 90 percent can not only do, but have a lot of fun doing.

We've come up with a saying that is *almost* biblical: "Where the Spirit of the Lord is, there is fun!" The low-risk, high-grace approach to outreach is something that anyone can do and keep on doing for life. And if we make it enjoyable enough, they'll bring their friends along with them!

A missionary e-mailed Steve from remote northern Thailand to say that he is doing servant evangelism by killing wild pigs and throwing feasts for the locals. He said entire villages are coming to Christ as a result of these acts of kindness. And a good time is being had by all!

Aha #2: Make It an Ongoing Process

The second big truth behind servant evangelism is that evangelism is a self-perpetuating, seasonal process. Paul made this clear when he wrote 1 Corinthians 3:6: "I planted the seed, Apollos watered it, but God made it grow." As we've noted a number of times in this book, the preharvesting aspects of evangelism are crucial. It is absolutely vital that we spend adequate time and attention planting, watering, and tending.

Recent evangelism techniques have overharvested. They've stripped the fields bare without giving proper attention to planting, watering, and tending crops for succeeding seasons. If all you do is harvest, there will never be another crop. Part of the reason for today's downturn in evangelistic results is that we've not valued or had patience for the processes that make evangelism work.

Aha #3: Make It Really Friendly Evangelism

Irresistible evangelism begins with an *attitude of acceptance.* All our efforts to love our city into relationship with Christ are for naught if we don't have something worthwhile to invite newcomers to once they've responded. We need to make sure we demonstrate a genuinely enjoyable party atmosphere when people come to check us out—*not* a perpetual funeral. All three of us have traveled extensively to speak at churches around the United States and abroad, and we've discovered that few churches know much about throwing a really welcoming party.

Countless churches have no passion, no variety, no fun. Activities are the same week in and week out, year after year. You've seen this happen in people's marriages, where a husband and wife are living under the same roof but have shut down emotionally. They broadcast a don't-bother-me vibe that is painful to be around. Churches do the same thing, sending a bad signal to people who come to check them out. Their inward focus conveys conditional acceptance: *Sure you're welcome here, as long as you dress like us…as long as you maintain a certain lifestyle…as long as you believe like us; otherwise just go away.* In other words, *You can all go to hell.*

> **CLEANING RESTROOMS**
> *(One- & two-person activity)*
>
> We roll up our sleeves and clean the scum off of toilets, mirrors, and sinks at gas stations and other places. "Why would you want to do that?" people might ask. Well, we think that if Jesus were around today he would be doing this—just as he washed his disciples' feet. People were surprised back then—and they're surprised today.

This is a great way to support the other projects, especially for people who are new to kindness outreaches and are a little nervous and wondering what it's all about. Prayer people focus on one of the projects and pray as others interact with community folks. The prayer people simply pray silently as they walk around the outreach site without drawing attention to themselves.

Do people have to believe in Jesus before they feel genuinely welcomed at your church? In most churches people would quickly answer, "No, unbelievers are always welcomed here." But the way they conduct business sends an entirely different message.[2]

With a little thought and preparation, we show the people coming into our churches that we're glad they're there. We can broadcast grace and acceptance by making everything easy to understand for folks who don't know the religious "ropes." For example, we should always introduce what's about to happen and how people might participate. The worship leader might say, "For the next fifteen to twenty minutes we're going to sing a few songs. The words will be projected on the screen. Feel free to stand up, sit down, or raise your hands as a gesture of worship. We want you to relate directly to God in the way that works for you."

We can also acknowledge a wide variety of opinions and lifestyles without necessarily approving of them. We can rejoice as much when a Marilyn Manson look-alike shows up as we do when someone comes in a sports jacket and tie. For many years Steve was so concerned that Vineyard Community Church might be alienating the "normal" middle class people that he gave all his messages wearing a loud tie and a conservative suit jacket.

Aha #4: Make It Immediate

The fourth and last big truth is that kindness evangelism is *best begun right now*. It's not a complex strategy that requires tons of training; you and your congregation can start doing this type of evangelism after a short briefing in which everybody learns to say, "We're washing cars for free to show God's love in a practical way." And, "No, we don't take donations. Think of someone you know who really needs the money, and go stick it in that person's mailbox!"

When it comes to evangelism, Christians often focus too much on preparation. We use it as a crutch or an excuse for inactivity. We are so absorbed in saying, "Ready, aim, ready, aim," that we never give a final command to fire! When it comes to kindness, we prefer, "Ready, fire! Aim." It may sound reckless to some, but wouldn't reckless kindness be a good thing? What if it got totally out of control and a chain-reaction happened so that thousands felt the love of Jesus? Perhaps "Fire! Fire! Fire!" would be an even better approach!

Kindness outreach can be personal and spontaneous: It can be volunteering to shovel snow, bag groceries at the supermarket, wash car windows at the self-serve gas station, or clean out rain gutters for the people in your neighborhood. It can also be a highly organized operation like Vineyard Community Church's Summer of Service, in which more than seven hundred teens from around the United States gather to do outreach. By day they go out into the city to do massive and diverse servant-evangelism projects. By night they gather for supercharged rock-and-roll worship.

These teens touch tens of thousands of people in the week they're together. It's amazing to watch the energy the kids expend and incredible to see the joy they receive from going out into the hot summer weather to do outreach. They come back day after day all charged up. When we ask them what drives them forward, they consistently say, "It's the look on people's faces when we tell them we're showing them God's love for free. It's beautiful every time!"

Every pastor knows that the largest attendance and the largest offering of the year typically come on Christmas Eve. We gather to celebrate the birth of the Savior Jesus, sing songs of the season, and light candles. It's all very cozy and touching. It's inspiring to see so many people with lit candles singing in one voice, but is it the best way of lifting up the name of Jesus? Steve tells how they broke tradition last year.

 We announced that we were going to do a kindness outreach on Christmas Eve. We mapped out over five hundred locations

where people might need a touch of God's love that night: fire houses, police stations, hospitals, and anywhere else we could think of. We distributed fourteen thousand Christmas doughnuts to teams of our people who gave them away in the community to show the love of Christ in a practical way. It was the first time many of our people personally talked to anybody about the love of Jesus. And it was great! We were all as giddy as a bunch of transformed Scrooges!

As the rehabilitated Ebenezer Scrooge demonstrated, Christmas is a season we must keep each day of the year. We must keep thinking up and giving away more and more simple gifts of kindness. One creative project that's had a great impact in the past couple of years is door-to-door car washes. Small teams pack up all the gear they need to do an in-driveway wash and then simply go knocking on doors with the offer of a free car wash.

On a lazy Saturday morning, it's a little surprising to have someone ring your doorbell and offer to wash your car for free. Most just start to laugh and say, "This is a joke, right?"

We just say, "No, this is for real. We are just showing Christ's love in a practical way. If Jesus were in town today, we think he would be doing practical things for people—maybe washing their cars."

At one house, the car-wash team couldn't help but notice a lot of screaming coming from behind the front door. The couple of the house was caught up in a shouting match that was impossible to miss. "You're nothing but a dirty little @#*&%!!" To that came a reply, "Oh, yeah? Well, you're worse than that. You're a *&^)-+=!!" At that point, one of the would-be car washers knocked on the door quite loudly.

"What do you want?"

"We're Christians, and we're here to wash your car for free to show you God's love in a practical way."

"Can't you hear that we're having a discussion?"

"Well, we'll just wash your car while you're having your discussion." (When it comes to showing God's love, we're persistent!)

GIVING GIFTS AT HOMES FOR SENIORS
(Larger-group activity)

This is a great activity for families with small children. We hand out hygienic items and interact with the residents at homes for seniors.

The team washed the two cars in the driveway and did a quality job. When they finished, they knocked on the door again to tell the lady of the house. She came to the door with a look of disbelief. She was visibly touched by the act of kindness that had been shown to her family. A team member asked, "Why don't we pray for you and your family?"

She got a little teary-eyed and said, "I think that's a wonderful idea." She assembled her entire family in a circle on the front lawn. When asked what they could pray for, the woman said, "Pray that we will continue on as a family. There are some forces at work that would like to see us torn apart." They all bowed in prayer.

The group from church prayed a simple prayer over the family: "Dear God, bring your peace to bear here in a strong way. Let your mercy rule over this family. In Christ's name, amen."

The whole family had tears in their eyes. It was apparent that God had been present, touching hearts.

Then someone in the circle suggested, "You know what? You ought to come to church with us tonight."

"Oh, we couldn't do that. Didn't you just hear us yelling at each other and carrying on like that? We couldn't come to church."

"Sure you could. You'd fit right in. There are lots of people just like you at our church."

"No way!"

"Yes way!"

"You meet us right by the south entrance, and we'll sit together. Then we'll go out afterward and have coffee."

The family was overwhelmed. They came that night, and they've been coming fairly regularly since then. To our knowledge none of them has made a faith commitment to Christ yet, but they're inching their way toward him. Frankly, we're OK with

WASHING CARS FOR FREE

(Larger group activity)

If the weather is favorable, we sometimes wash cars for free—no donations accepted! That always gets people's attention. They wonder why we're doing it if we're not raising money for something. "Well," we explain, "we're just letting people know that God loves them and that his love is free."

Here are a few simple responses to use when someone asks why you're doing the outreach.

"We're just trying to show God's love in a practical way."

"It's free to show you that God's love is free!"

"We think if Jesus were here today this is something he would do."

"We are not about 'marketing' any particular church. We give connection cards so that people can connect if they desire, but our goal is simply to present Christ in a tangible way by expressing his grace, love, and mercy. "

For a listing of a lot more projects and insights on how to do them, check out our Web site: www.servantevangelism.com.

that. We're trusting the Holy Spirit to keep working.

We like this story—partly because it closes without a complete ending. The people didn't all get saved and have everything turn out great for them from then on. They haven't arrived, but they're on their way. They're still in mid-sentence. Their needs are being addressed, and they're beginning to open their hearts to God. Now they need Christian friends who'll take the time to listen well enough and long enough to help them navigate the next stage on their journey toward God. That's the topic of our next chapter.

ENDNOTES

1. "But love your enemies, do good to them, and lend to them without expecting to get anything back. Then your reward will be great, and you will be sons of the Most High, because he is kind to the ungrateful and wicked" (Luke 6:35).

2. Check out *Community of Kindness* by Steve Sjogren and Rob Lewin (Ventura, CA: Regal Books, 2003). It is all about how to create an environment of acceptance in the local church, and it offers more than one hundred ideas about how to think through the invitation process.

CHAPTER 7

Active
FRIENDSHIP

> "Give every man thine ear, but few thy voice."
> —WILLIAM SHAKESPEARE,
> *Hamlet*

> "Therefore consider carefully how you listen."
> —LUKE 8:18

A few years ago Steve called Dave from Germany, where he was in the midst of a highly successful European servant evangelism tour: "Could you send a team of people over here to teach listening skills to everyone we train? Our students are seeing great results, but once the people they're reaching start showing up in church, they're not going to want to stay—not unless these Christians get much better at listening."

In golfing terms, acts of kindness move the ball far down the fairway, but moving the ball to the green requires the listening and friendship skills necessary to enter another person's world.

Larry Chrouch, one of the pastors in charge of outreach at Vineyard Community Church, says, "Practicing evangelism without listening is like playing golf blindfolded—any results you achieve are probably accidental."

Since Steve and his colleagues first began training leaders to do kindness outreach back in the 1980s, they've been encouraging people to take *Listening for Heaven's Sake* training from Equipping Ministries International[1] as their first step toward effective follow-up. Anyone who wants to lead a small group at Vineyard Community Church is expected to take EMI's basic relationship-training courses first. The principles learned in this course help not-yet-Christians feel genuinely valued and respected, and they keep all of the leaders healthier and prevent them from burning out.

Dave likes to say that helping church members learn to listen effectively is like giving your church a broad-spectrum (relational) antibiotic. It can prevent power struggles, and it can keep the germs of misunderstanding from gaining a foothold and causing a world of hurt for everyone involved. The demands of operating an outwardly focused church are extreme enough without additional stresses caused by harmful relationship dynamics. Listening training also helps get rid of the irrational pressure that leaders feel to constantly dispense "right answers" and replaces that pressure with a humble determination to show Christlike warmth, understanding, and respect. Basically the training helps us learn how to "be there" for people who need us.

In today's spiritual environment, listening isn't merely a pastoral counseling tool to be used with people who have marital problems. Effective listening is an essential ingredient without which all ministry is powerless. Without effective listening, people and leaders alike stay stuck in a fruitless and frustrating succession of head-to-head monologues. Unlike some Christians we know who delight in butting heads over competing worldviews, most of today's pre-Christian seekers would rather avoid the headache. They're likely to respond far more positively to people who take the time to understand them.

LISTENING OPENS DOORS

Jan and one of her fellow Athletes in Action staffers had just taken EMI's listening course when they had a wonderful chance to use the skills they'd learned. They were unwinding in a hotel whirlpool when two adolescent girls joined them in the tub. One of the teens, named Brittany, began passionately telling her friend about an upcoming Wiccan[2] gathering that she was planning to attend. Jan says:

Normally we would have tried to counter the girl's ideas, but we decided to listen instead. I said something simple like, "Wow, you really sound excited about this!" This was all the encouragement she needed to launch into a five-minute explanation of why she was so attracted to neo-pagan rituals. The bottom line was that she'd had a really traumatic time in high school and the Wiccas accepted her. She said, "I've gone through so much crap just trying to make it through high school that I'll probably be in therapy for the rest of my life!"

I tried to mirror back what she said with, "It's hard for you to even imagine a future where you'd be free from all of the pain you've gone through."

What came next completely floored me. With a film of tears starting to form in her eyes and with complete sincerity in her voice, she said, "Sometimes I wish I could be born all over again. I'd really like to start over from scratch." After a long pause, my friend asked if she would really like to be born again. "Yes, I really would," she said.

It seems that the power of the Holy Spirit works through us so much better when we slow down and listen. We must sacrifice to put our agendas aside and tune in to God's heart for another person, but this genuine surrender of time and effort opens hearts and can awaken an irresistible hunger to find and to know our God.

In a recent weekly Leadership Journal Internet poll,[3] pastors were asked, "How have you adapted the way you share your faith in our changing culture?" The number-one response (24 percent) was "I listen more, even when I strongly disagree." The number-two response (22 percent) was "I now see evangelism as a longer process." Other answers included "I'm not as preachy as I used to be" (14 percent), and "I've stopped using tracts, 'laws,' and 'plans' " (12 percent).

More and more leaders are beginning to realize the value of seeking to understand before working to be understood. Let's take a look at the impact listening had on one ordinary person in the midst of her search for God.

Looking for Unconditional Love

Her mother was an alcoholic, and her father was distant and critical toward his five children. Throughout her formative years, Melinda felt no tenderness or parental affection. As the oldest, she felt tremendous guilt and extreme pressure to be a "good girl" and a role model for the rest of the kids.

My family was very involved in church when I was a child, and I got many years of comfort there. It was a refuge for me. I would spend as much time there as possible, trying to escape what was happening at home. But as I grew older, the message I got from church sounded more and more like the "be a good girl or you'll be punished" message I was getting at home. I vividly remember meeting with a pastor who told me that God couldn't possibly love me because I was so full of sin. What I heard was that there was something terrible inside me that made me undesirable and unacceptable to God. I don't know what I'd done that was so wrong, but apparently I wasn't a good enough girl!

By the time I was ready to leave home and go to college, I could feel a tremendous rage building inside me. I was sick of being good and furious with my parents and their God for being so distant and demanding. I rebelled with a vengeance. In college and graduate school, I tried anything and everything that promised freedom. I was really wild, really depressed, and really disappointed. I felt so anxious and hopeless that I began seeing a therapist and was eventually hospitalized for severe depression.

I loved the hospital. The patients there completely accepted me. It was the first place I'd ever been where it was OK to be messed up. I'd never experienced such unconditional caring from anyone in my life. My stay was over far too soon, but when I left there, I entered into the most joyful and productive period of my life. It lasted until I met my husband.

Although we were together for many years, things started to go wrong soon after we married. He would withdraw and turn increasingly distant and self-absorbed. I would wear myself out trying to get through to him and involve him in our marriage. Gradually we became more and more disconnected until one day he left me. Within weeks of our separation, he began seeing a younger woman.

After the divorce, it seemed I had nothing to live for. It was the most painful and disappointing thing that ever happened to me. I'd screwed up my life, and nothing I could think of would fix it. I became despondent and suicidal. That's when my friend Sarah invited me to Divorce and Beyond,[4] a group that met in her church. She'd already spent hours listening to me and talking me back from the edge of despair. Since I trusted her and I knew she'd been through a divorce herself, I was ready to give it a try.

I was a little shaky about going to a meeting in a church, but I was quickly reassured by the accepting, nonjudgmental attitudes of the people there. The group leader, Mark, was really sensitive and did a great job, listening and including everyone in the conversation. When he began talking about how God loves everyone unconditionally in a way we could never find in people, I started to cry—a lot. This had never happened to me before. It was like he was looking right into my heart.

I'm actually kind of embarrassed recounting this, but in that moment I had a visual impression of a sword of pure light piercing right through my solar plexus. I saw the emotional layers inside me parting

like ribs spreading and revealing an empty space at the very core of me.
I was terrified, but it wasn't a bad kind of terrified that made me want
to run away. Somehow I knew what Mark was saying was just for me,
that I was in the right place, and that maybe, just maybe, the God
Mark was talking about might really care for me unconditionally.

I still have many questions that I hope will be answered by the
Alpha⁵ class I'm taking. I question some of the cultural aspects of the
Bible and the anti-woman stance I hear from so many Christians, but
what keeps drawing me back is the way the people at Sarah's church
keep listening and giving. I don't understand or agree with everything
they say, but I'm beginning to think and feel that finding the God of
unconditional love might be possible for me—and it might be easier
than I ever dreamed.

LISTENING TO PRE-CHRISTIANS

Until Melinda's friend Sarah began reaching out to her, she was part of a large and growing crowd of people who, though somewhat interested in spiritual things, have turned their backs on organized religion. They've already checked out "church" and have made up their minds that it's not what they're looking for. They've had bad experiences or acquired their views from watching flamboyant televangelists or made up their minds based on the "barroom theology" bantered back and forth anywhere opinionated people gather. However they've come to their conclusion, Christians have been "weighed and found wanting."

So the real question now becomes, How can we "un-make up" their minds? We've discussed how acts of kindness can work to attract a fresh second look, but by themselves they are not enough to bring folks close enough to embrace a relationship with God. That takes a much more individualized approach. A large majority (72 percent) of respondents to a survey conducted by the Gallup organization said they view spirituality as a highly personal and individual affair rather than a matter of religion or church doctrine.⁶

And there is nothing more individual and attractive than telling your story to someone who cares enough to genuinely listen.

It's important to realize that people like Melinda aren't usually interested in church or even consciously looking for God at first. Though they may hunger for a spiritual connection in a vague sort of way, what they're often deliberately looking for are practical ways to meet their basic needs. They want to reduce their pain or to cope with loneliness and stress. Or maybe they're seeking ways to control unruly kids or to strengthen their marriages. Individual needs vary so greatly from one person to the next that no generic set of recovery programs or felt-needs curricula could ever address them all.

Recovery programs are terrific, and we highly recommend them, but they can never completely meet a person's emotional and relational needs. That takes lots of *real* people who *really* know how to listen. At VCC we are always working hard to develop what Dr. Henry Cloud and Dr. John Townsend call safe people.[7] These are the kind of people who befriend others without trying to manipulate or control them. They come alongside pre-Christians and seasoned Christ-followers alike. They pay attention and show love in ways that draw everyone closer to God.

LISTENING SAND TRAPS

Very few people are openly opposed to listening. We know it is a good thing, like prayer and good stewardship. It's good for us like the Brussels sprouts or broccoli our mothers made us eat as children. Many leaders respond to the idea of listening with the same enthusiasm that a hyperactive four-year-old has for naptime. We acknowledge the theoretical need for it but steer clear of situations where we have to put it into practice.

Steve explains that most pastors have been carefully taught and thoroughly conditioned to be parental toward the people they meet.

We see our job as teaching and correcting people. We're supposed to know how to warn them when they're going down the wrong path. It's very difficult to sit back and listen to people drone on and on about their difficulties when I'm thinking, If they'd just shut up and listen to me, I'd show them a principle or two about how to live their lives more effectively. Then they'd be much more successful! If I take a step back and look at this attitude from a more objective standpoint, it's easy to see how egotistical and conceited it is.

For a while, being a kind of cosmic Shell Answer Man may pump up your sense of self-importance, but it's a bad deal for everyone involved. It doesn't truly help people, and it sets you up for a serious ego-correcting fall. These days I'm learning that the more humbly I listen to people, the better I can hear God.

I have grown much in my listening skills in the past few years since my accident, but when I meet a person who is stuck in a no-win situation, I still long to teach. That's why when I speak at church, I find the most challenging part of the morning is the ten minutes immediately after the message is over.

People come up front and want to share their life problems with me. In my pre-accident days, I would let them talk for a few seconds and then bend down to give them the most extensive and well-reasoned spiritual prescription I could think up on the spot. Back then, I would do most of the talking. Now I am turning the tables. I am laying aside my agenda and trying to listen from my heart. As I lay my life down and listen to the individual in front of me, I end up having far greater insight and a greater impact on each individual in much less time. God increases when I decrease!

As Steve points out, there are obstacles we must overcome if we want to listen in a way that opens spiritual doors. Dave points to five behaviors that inhibit and even destroy the spiritual connection between people looking for spiritual answers and ourselves. Think of them as relational "sand traps" that we need to avoid if we want to get to the green. Usually we are not consciously aware of them or the negative impact they are having on our relationships and our outreach.

IMPATIENCE

The first obstacle, and perhaps most difficult to overcome, is what John Ortberg calls "spiritual attention-deficit disorder." As we've said, when people are seeking, they aren't usually aware that they're looking for God. They are in pain or in love or trying to find their way out of some crisis in their lives. What they really want and need in those stressful times is evidence that we care and are giving them our full attention.

Just as physical attention-deficit disorder causes many school children to have great difficulty in completing their academic coursework, spiritual attention-deficit disorder makes it hard for us to complete the relational ministry assignments God gives to us. We may genuinely want to show people the compassion of Jesus, but being human means we all have to overcome this universal distractibility disability.

There are a number of reasons we quickly lose patience when other people are talking. Instead of carefully following what is being said, we may be hurriedly formulating brilliant responses that will make us look clever. We may be multi-tasking—listening with one small part of our brain while planning the rest of the day's busy agenda with the rest. We may be internally fuming and nonverbally prompting the speaker to hurry up and get on with the story.

Even if we are somewhat dull mentally, our brains process information ten to twenty times faster than anyone can talk. Listening requires spending a good bit of time mentally waiting around. Patience, the art of being hopeful and peaceful while you wait, is a fruit of the Spirit that must be painstakingly cultivated. It takes discipline to quiet the internal racket that distracts us.

Instead of fidgeting, half-listening, or giving the highly resistible Mister Fix-It answer that intelligent people like Melinda naturally resent, you can dial down and dial deeper. As C.S. Lewis pointed out so eloquently in *The Weight of Glory*, other than the sacrament of the Lord's Supper, the spirit of the human being to whom you're talking is perhaps the holiest thing you will ever encounter. So take off your shoes as Moses did at the burning bush. Treat the conversation with sacred seriousness and Christlike calm.

Connecting with seekers like Brittany and Melinda requires listening well enough to understand them and long enough to help them feel safe as they unfold their stories. Of course, you do not have unlimited time, but how much time are you and the people of your church willing to invest so people can feel heard? When seekers detect that you are impatient with listening, they take it as a signal to give up and go away or, worse, to suck it up and try to please you. Either way, the respect and the caring connection are damaged.

JUMPING TO CONCLUSIONS OR CAUSES

Another challenge we face in learning how to listen in a way that opens hearts is our tendency to jump to conclusions and causes. We start off by tracking with what is being said, but then we wander on ahead to where we think the speaker is going. We assume we've gotten a good enough read on the seeker's bottom-line belief to understand it without listening any further. We just mentally zip ahead to (what is in our mind) an obvious conclusion based on our experiences, preconceptions, and prejudices. Even when we are right, most people sense that we've made up our minds and stopped listening. If you've ever been in a conversation with someone who jumped to conclusions about you, you know how rude and disrespectful it feels.

When pre-Christians call us narrow-minded, they are usually reacting to their experiences of feeling prejudged before their ideas were given a fair hearing. *Jumping to cause* is presuming to know the deeper motivations that are causing anyone to say, do, or believe certain things. We think, *You're just saying that because you're Jewish,* or *You just think that because you're uneducated,* or *You're just being difficult because you're a woman!*

Stereotyping and negatively categorizing people's motives instead of hearing them out is extraordinarily offensive to anyone with healthy self-esteem. When people detect that this is what we're doing, any constructive connection that may have been building is quite likely to end abruptly.

We're rarely aware of how this blunder feels unless we are on the receiving end of it. A friend of Dave's was interviewing an African-American woman who was being considered to head a program for pregnant teens. He stunned everyone in the room by asking her, "How do we know that you aren't going to steal money from the program like Jim [a former employee] did?" After a painful pause, she pointed out that the only thing she had in common with Jim was the color of her skin. Without realizing it, Dave's friend revealed that he thought that one of the traits that leads to stealing is being an African American. To his credit, he apologized profusely and asked for help with overcoming the racist attitudes that his *jumping to cause* had brought to light.

PATRONIZING

It is tempting to view pre-Christians, or anyone looking for help, as not quite as bright or functional as we are. We are the wise and gifted helpers, and they are the huddled masses yearning to be free. Because we don't always speak the same language, we assume they must be more needy and not quite as intelligent as we are, but of course, that's not true. Most seekers are much more sophisticated than we imagine. We can't say enough here about the need to communicate genuine respect to each person Jesus deemed worthy of offering himself for. Assuming we possess all of the answers needed to easily fix the hurts and pains of others is not only arrogant but abhorrent to many seekers. God is all-knowing, but we are not.

Condescending attitudes demean people's intelligence by treating them as if they were children. Their spiritual experiences may differ from ours, but we needn't talk down to them as if we are the smart spiritual grown-ups assigned to tutor low-functioning kids. The best way to treat anybody seeking help is spelled out in Philippians 2:3: "Do nothing out of selfish ambition or vain conceit, but in humility consider others better than yourselves." We don't just listen to be helpful; we presuppose that everyone we meet has something of profound value to teach us about life.

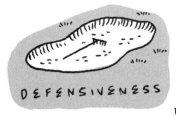

DEFENSIVENESS

One of the sad truths that explains why many people who love Jesus don't care to listen or talk to pre-Christian people is that we are frightened by the very thought of spending time with unbelievers. We've been told since we were children to stay away from "those people"; they're a bad influence. They bring bad spiritual juju that could rub off on us—and besides, they really don't like us. Somehow it's our job to save them, and we feel guilty because we don't know how. No wonder we feel anxious and defensive!

It's hard to listen when you're afraid and suspicious, because you think you have to protect yourself. Defensiveness on our part naturally breeds more defensiveness in the hearts of those we would reach. If you walk into a room filled with unbelieving family members and are "loaded for bear," ready to whip out your biblical apologetics and arguments for faith at the first sign of resistance, it should come as no surprise when they fight you. It quickly becomes a shouting match with each side saying, "I'm right!" and "No, you're not! I'm right!"

The only cure we know for defensiveness is to lay down your agenda for a while. Take the advice of that old camp song "Down by the Riverside": "I'm gonna lay down my sword and shield, down by the riverside." Instead of desperately trying to defend your point of view, try really working to understand how others think, feel, and believe. If your faith is real, listening to their arguments won't harm you. It won't matter if you don't have any zinger comebacks if you cease (at least temporarily) trying to prove how wrong they are. If they ask a good question, you can always say, "That's a good question; I'll have to give that some thought."

The worst thing that can happen is that you will have to do some real thinking about what you believe. And that's always a good thing! Arguing about faith doesn't usually produce fruit, but listening opens hearts. If our hearts are open to God and to those we hope to nudge closer to God, great things can happen.

We've found that most people aren't nearly as concerned with our answers as they are with being treated as if they are valuable and important. The question isn't so much "What would Jesus say?" as "What would he do?" If your answer is that he would confront them, it may be helpful to go back and look at the Scriptures. The people Jesus confronted most often and most vigorously were the religious people who thought they already knew all the answers, not the seekers!

CODEPENDENCY

If we want to do what Jesus did, it helps to think as Jesus thinks. We can't have unhealthy motives and twisted relationships and expect to see great fruit for the kingdom of heaven. That's why the last obstacle we will touch on is unhealthy codependency. It may seem like an odd topic for a book on evangelism, but this kind of thinking cripples evangelistic relationships and makes everyone miserable. In this context, codependency means fostering relationships in which we take inappropriate responsibility for another's thoughts, feelings, beliefs, or behavior.

Parents fall into these patterns with their growing children, wives with their husbands, siblings and friends with each other. Whenever we attempt to persuade people by manipulating them—inducing fear, shame, or guilt—even to rescue them, our behavior is codependent. In *The Message*, Eugene Peterson paraphrases Romans 14:22–23, saying:

"Cultivate your own relationship with God, but don't impose it on others. You're fortunate if your behavior and belief are coherent. But if you're not sure, if you notice that you're acting in ways inconsistent with what you believe—some days trying to impose your opinions on others, other days trying to please them—then you know you're out of line."

No matter how much we love another person, that person's choices are up to him or her. The person alone is responsible and accountable to God. Our job is to be consistently open, caring, and honest.

In Matthew 19:16-22, we read the story of Jesus and a young man who was clearly seeking. He asked, "Teacher, what good thing must I do to get eternal life?" After telling Jesus that he had kept all of the commandments of that law, he asked, " 'What do I still lack?' Jesus answered, 'If you want to be perfect [whole and healthy], go, sell your possessions and give to the poor, and you will have treasure in heaven. Then come, follow me.' When the young man heard this, he went away sad, because he had great wealth."

This doesn't sound very "seeker friendly" in codependent ears. The young man was so close! Why did Jesus make such a difficult demand? If he really loved the young man, wouldn't he go after him? Our best guess is that Jesus really *did* love the young man and that's why he was utterly honest with him. Jesus wanted to be sure that the young man knew that, for him, the price of following would be giving up his bondage to wealth. Jesus didn't take it upon himself to scare him or sweet-talk him or argue him into agreement. He left the choice squarely on the young man's shoulders where it rightfully belonged.

No matter how painful it is to watch people make choices we don't like, it's unhealthy to try to control them or allow their unhealthy choices to control us.

It is difficult to allow people this costly kind of freedom and respect. We want to rescue them from themselves. We hate to watch them walk away and turn their backs on God. But if Jesus did it, it must be a good and loving thing to do. It must be better to be painstakingly honest about what the real choices are than to cajole or plead or manipulate. No matter how painful it is to watch people make choices we don't like, it's unhealthy to try to control them or allow their unhealthy choices to control us.

The radical mercy of God is twofold. He allows us the privilege of freely choosing or rejecting him, but he leaves the door open and the light on to receive any returning prodigals who change their minds.

It's hard to respect the choices of people who from our perspective are recklessly disregarding the life preservers we try to toss their way. It's tempting to try to drag them, kicking and screaming, against their will. This is the prime reason we commit most of the deadly sins of evangelism mentioned in earlier chapters. On the other hand, good evangelistic listening recognizes and respects the spiritual addresses where the people we care about have taken up residence. We are always tuned in to where they're coming from even when we don't like it. Years before his death, composer Rich Mullins penned a song for a friend who at the time was choosing to reject Jesus. The chorus spells out the reality of the situation as Rich saw it:

You can live without Him...if you want.
You can turn your back on music...Turn your back on love.
You can live without Him...if you want.
But that is so much less than I could ever choose.

© January 2002, mullinsongs[8]

Dave and several of Rich's friends believe that this is one of his finest songs. Even though he was one of the top-selling contemporary Christian artists of the last twenty years, evangelical record labels have refused to record it. Some thought it was too depressing and that it was wrong to tell people that they could, in fact, choose to live without Jesus. As painful as it sounds, it's a good and healthy thing to recognize the reality and necessity of choice—even when we are hoping and praying that our friends and loved ones will choose, as Rich's friend eventually did, to give their hearts to Jesus.

When you genuinely love someone and are invested in the outcome of his or her choices, respecting that person's desires can be especially difficult. Dave relates the story of how for five years he had been persistently courting Pam, his friend and lay-counseling partner. For about two of those five years, he proposed to her once every three weeks. After a while, she told him to stop asking. He found it hard to honor her wishes, but he kept his mouth shut. One day as they were having lunch together after a session, she said, "If you had asked me to marry you this week, I would have said 'yes.' " This is what Dave had been praying for all along, but he had to ask what had changed her mind. She replied, "I decided that I could live without you, *but I don't want to!*"

That choice is the goal of healthy evangelistic listening. Even though we know that folks can choose an eternity separated from God, we want to connect with their hearts and demonstrate his love in such a way that they won't want to live without him.

Much of good evangelistic listening consists of not stumbling over the five obstacles we've described, but there are also two somewhat counterintuitive listening habits that will help you connect deeply with those you wish to reach.

LISTENING WITH YOUR EYES

Irresistible evangelists practice the *ministry of noticing*—picking up on hundreds of tiny nuances and minor details that speak volumes about what is happening inside other people. By paying special attention to messages sent by a person's eyes, nonverbal gestures, and overall posture, we can tune into a seeker's deep heart. Whenever Steve visits a new city to lead an outreach, he likes to walk around the local shopping malls with a cup of coffee in his hand. He watches the people around him very carefully. He looks intently into their eyes and asks himself, "What do I hear?"

God spoke to me early on in my ministry and told me that if I looked into people's eyes—with his help—I could see where they're hurting. It's not mystical or magical; he made us all with this ability. If you watch closely enough, hidden pain, worry, and hope are all there to see. This is how I get the 'feel' of what makes a person or a whole city tick so I can discern the best ways to reach out.

On the flip side, we need to consider what our own eyes and nonverbal gestures say to those we listen to. Are we sending messages of welcome and understanding? Are we wordlessly saying, "You're somebody who really matters"? Or are we unconsciously transmitting the message that they are bothering and annoying us? Listening with our eyes involves both receiving and sending lots of these little signals. This requires more focus and effort than most people find convenient, but this is one of the costs of building trust. Eugene Peterson's paraphrase of Romans 15:1-3 in *The Message* puts it this way:

"Those of us who are strong and able in the faith need to step in and lend a hand to those who falter, and not just do what is convenient for us. Strength is for service not status. Each one of us needs to look after the good of the people around us, asking ourselves, 'How can I help?' That's exactly what Jesus did. He didn't make it easy for himself by avoiding people's troubles, but waded right in and helped out."

SEEING WITH YOUR EARS

This Christlike ministry of paying attention means we must also take what people are saying very seriously. The best way to do this is by concentrating very closely on the three basic layers of messages people are communicating. No matter what people are talking about, these three major components are always present: (1) the ideas they are talking about, (2) the feelings they are expressing verbally or nonverbally, and (3) the bottom-line beliefs that are driving their thoughts and feelings.

For instance, the story Melinda told (earlier in this chapter) about her spiritual search contained a good bit of detail. On the idea level, she said that she came to the Divorce and Beyond group because her friend Sarah invited her. On the feeling level, she expressed tremendous fear, hurt, disappointment, and anger toward God and the church. She also expressed feelings of trust toward Sarah and Mark. The bottom-line beliefs she was struggling with related to whether the Christian God really loves her in the unconditional way she has always wanted so desperately.

Most of us are at least aware of the skills that have come to be called *active listening*. They are taught in most counseling courses and are now an increasingly common part of most business communication training. We may understand the theory and may have even memorized reflective listening formulas such as "It sounds as if you feel...about such and such." Some dismiss this teaching as a secular and artificial technique while others embrace what they've learned and use it in counseling work. In his ministry with EMI, Dave has worked with other relational ministry pioneers to integrate good biblical theology and practical listening skills.

In my experience, the most effective evangelists are the ones who use active listening in a respectful way that allows them to see into the deep-heart beliefs of seekers. I've seen amazing evangelistic fruit from good listening. One of my former students, a training director for a major international evangelistic ministry tells me, "Godly listening skills turn otherwise ordinary Christians into 'seeker magnets' who draw people into relationship with Christ." He is now requiring all staff to learn and practice these skills.

A good evangelistic listener is a person who inspires trust so that people not only allow access to their world, but find they can take a deeper look into places they would probably avoid otherwise. Serving and listening go together and will help take us a long way, but there are more exciting evangelistic skills yet to come. The next chapter focuses on a skill set you've probably never heard of—the art of active wondering.

Listening *for a* connection

Choose someone you would like to know better. Fill in this form to see how well you really know him or her.

Name:

Occupation:

Family members:

Interests:

Whether you're relating to a relative, a neighbor, a friend, or a co-worker, the more you know about the person's likes, dislikes, anxieties, and hopes, the easier it will be to connect to his or her world with God's love.

Listen and observe, then fill in the blanks to the right as you think the person would.

Any answers you don't know can serve as opportunities to listen more and to grow in your relationship.

Listening and praying will open a connection for the Holy Spirit to work through.

FAVORITE	LEAST FAVORITE	WORRIES	DREAMS
Music CDs	Music	World affairs	Ideal job
Foods	Meals	Economy	
Restaurants	Colors	Job	Ideal vacation
Movies	Celebrities		
Books	Relatives	Finances	Ideal relationship
TV shows	Co-workers	Friendships	
Hobbies	Parts of the day	Family	Deepest wish
Sports	Season of the year		
Holidays	Attitudes	Love life	
Heroes	Habits	Physical health	Secret ambition
Accomplishments	Philosophies	Emotional life	
Conversation topics	Peeves	Life direction	Miracles needed
Birthday gifts	Life events		
Way to relax and unwind	Jobs	Spiritual life	

Endnotes

1. This ten-hour course is available though Equipping Ministries International. To get more information about Listening for Heaven's Sake and other practical relationship training courses, visit their Web site at www.equipmin.org or call their toll free number: 1-800-364-4769.

2. Wicca is a neo-pagan religion that mingles elaborate rituals, spells, witchcraft, and nature worship.

3. Leadership Journal's Internet poll (www.leadershipjournal.net) from February 26, 2003.

4. Divorce and Beyond is a special seminar designed to reach out to anyone who has gone through divorce. It is followed by a fifteen-week small group. For more information, contact the Vineyard Community Church in Cincinnati at www.cincyvineyard.com.

5. The Alpha Course is a fifteen-session program that runs over ten weeks to provide seekers with an opportunity to explore the meaning of life and a practical introduction to the Christian faith. For more information, contact www.alphacourse.org. In the evangelistic golfing terms discussed in Chapter 5, we think Alpha works best as people approach the green.

6. George Gallup Jr. and Timothy Jones, *The Next American Spirituality: Finding God in the 21st Century* (Colorado Springs: Cook Communications, 2000), 50.

7. In *Safe People* (Grand Rapids, MI: Zondervan, 1995), Drs. Cloud and Townsend offer solid guidance for making safe choices in relationships. They help identify the nurturing people we all need in our lives, as well as ones we need to learn to avoid.

8. "You Can Live Without Him" by Richard Mullins. © 1979 mullinsongs (ASCAP) (administered by The Loving Company). All rights reserved. Used by permission. Many of Rich Mullins' previously unpublished songs are now being made available to serious recording artists from the Mullins Family Foundation, under the mullinsongs copyright.

CHAPTER 8

Active WONDERING

> "Wonder is the basis of worship."
>
> —THOMAS CARLYLE

> "As soon as all the people saw Jesus, they were overwhelmed with wonder and ran to greet him."
>
> —MARK 9:15

Doug was dead tired. He'd crisscrossed the country, leading his team in seven exhibition basketball games in as many days. As he sank into his seat on the airplane for the homeward flight, he let out a massive, internal sigh of relief. Doug relates:

> *I had waited until everyone in the boarding area got on the plane before boarding the plane myself. I wanted to be the last person on so I could drop into a seat where I could be alone and grab some shut-eye. But after I sat down, I saw one last person hurrying down the aisle with her luggage. I prayed, "Lord, please don't let that person sit next to me!" Not only did she plunk down right next to me, but within seconds it was clear that she was a major extrovert.*
>
> *I had to make a choice. My tired body was screaming for sleep, but I sensed that the Lord was calling me to engage my seat mate in conversation. I've learned over the years that some of the most Spirit-led conversations are*

the ones that happen when I'm at my worst. So I jumped in. She was more than ready to share her story. As I listened, she told me a lot about herself and, especially, about her passionate interest in art.

I said, "I don't know much about art, but I'm wondering what artistic success would look like for you. What do you want to do with your talent?" She told me she wanted to move to Santa Fe, New Mexico, and open a shop that catered to the thriving artist community there. Then after an anguished pause, she added, "I haven't told anyone else about this, but I've been seriously considering leaving my husband and children so I can move to Santa Fe to pursue my dream."

Now I was awake. I realized that God had used my willingness to listen to create an opportunity to touch her life in a significant way. So I said something like, "Wow, you're looking at making a decision that could change the whole direction of your life."

She nodded her agreement and began explaining her arguments in favor of walking away from her marriage and her family. After a while, I interjected, saying, "When I'm thinking through a big decision, I like to imagine forward about the future my choices might produce." Then I asked, "If you were to fast-forward to your life at age sixty-five, how do you think this decision might have played out?"

She thought for a minute, then said, "I would probably be wealthy, and I'd be fulfilled professionally. I'd be living in the place of my dreams—but I'd be lonely and bitter because I would have sacrificed

99 WONDERING QUESTIONS

THAT COULD WORK FOR YOU

Our belief is that we're never more than three good questions away from a breakthrough conversation with someone we're trying to build a bridge to, so we've grouped these wondering questions in sets of three. The important thing to remember about wondering questions, though, is the context in which they're asked. We need to pray for an opening door so that our questions can touch the hearts of those with whom we seek to connect. In the right context and with the right attitude and atmosphere, any of these ninety-nine questions can be powerful tools. But the best questions always come from the wondering that the Holy Spirit is stirring inside of you.

my family to get there. On the other hand, if I stay with my husband, I'll spend the next fourteen years raising kids and regretting that I never had the guts to fulfill myself. Neither one of these options is any good! What do you think I should do?"

I took a few seconds to gather my thoughts and then said, "To be honest, when I'm facing big, confusing choices, I pray to God to give me the wisdom I lack. It's amazing how much insight I get when I remember to pray."

She smiled wistfully and said, "You're a Christian, aren't you? You know, back in high school, I was in a group called Young Life where we used to pray and talk about God all the time. Those were the happiest days of my life!"

For the next hour and a half, the woman talked to Doug about her desire to return to the faith she'd left back in high school. As the flight arrived at its destination, she asked Doug to come with her to talk to her husband who was there to meet her. They hit it off immediately and conversed for a good while. In the end, the couple thanked Doug again and again for caring enough to listen and reach out. As he headed for home, Doug was wide awake and incredibly excited about the way God had used his simple questions to help change the direction of a whole family.

Wouldn't it be great if all our questions were so well received

---

LIFE LESSONS

A. I've made it my lifelong goal to learn from others; what's the greatest lesson you've learned thus far in your life's journey?

B. Tell me about your greatest success and your greatest failure along the way.

C. Would you share the greatest piece of wisdom ever passed on to you?

LIFE GOALS

A. What prompted you to pursue your career in _____?

B. What do you like most about what you do; how about the least?

C. Do you see what you're doing as a lifetime career or a stepping-stone to something else?

GOD

A. If someone wanted to talk to you about God, how would you like to be approached?

B. Has anyone ever approached you and tried to talk to you about God?

C. What kinds of feelings were you left with after the encounter?

and created such a positive impact? Perhaps you're assuming that what Doug did is something that just comes naturally to outgoing people. Nothing could be further from the truth. If Doug had done what comes naturally, the conversation would not have started in the first place. Let's take a closer look at the practical principles of irresistible evangelism that were in play.

Doug's simple inquiries worked wonders because they flowed from a willingness to listen compassionately without judging. As he followed the Spirit's leading, he very quickly began to discern the woman's spiritual address. She was very open and actively seeking *direction* for her life. In terms of the golf analogy we've been using, she was far down the fairway and approaching the green. Even though initially Doug was a reluctant listener, God's compassion shone through him so that she sensed genuine interest coming from a safe and caring person. At first, as so often happens, she gave no indication of the depth of her need or that, ultimately, hers was a spiritual quest. Soon, however, she decided to trust Doug enough to reveal her deepest thoughts. As she did so, Doug began using the question-asking skills we've dubbed active wondering.

IN TOUCH WITH YOUR WONDER

We've seen how God used Doug's genius for asking questions

EVANGELISM

A. What images or words come to your mind when you hear the word *evangelism*?

B. The word *evangelism* means proclaiming good news; why do you think so many people view this word so negatively?

C. Do you know what the good news is that evangelists are supposed to be sharing with people?

CAREER

A. What is your ultimate vocational dream?

B. What stands in the way of your achieving it?

C. What advice would you give to a young person just entering the workforce today?

RELIGIOUS EXPERIENCE

A. What kind of exposure did you have to religion as you were growing up?

B. Why do you think there are so many different religions?

C. Do you think it's possible for each one to be right?

and wondering aloud to open doors for a woman who felt lost, but did you know that you have that same ability within you? The great scientist and philosopher Buckminster Fuller liked to say that we are all born geniuses, but life has a way of "de-genius-izing" us. Peer pressure and cultural demands rob most adults of the awe, amazement, and curiosity God gives us as children. We're born with an outstanding ability for wondering, but somewhere along the way we learn that wondering isn't the accepted grown-up thing to do. We stop wondering aloud because we're afraid of looking stupid and being judged negatively. We read between the lines and discover that wondering is dangerous and perhaps even a menace to the status quo.

Wondering questions can lead to unconventional solutions that shake things up and turn our worlds upside down. Jesus practiced a revolutionary way of wondering aloud that changed lives and infuriated the religious leaders of his day. Even though he knew everything, he was always wondering. For example, he wondered about the contradictions between the way religious leaders kept the Sabbath and who they said he was. He encouraged his followers to wonder about God by telling them thought-provoking stories about unjust judges and annoying neighbors who borrowed bread in the middle of the night.

But Jesus couldn't have endorsed wondering more strongly than when he said, "Let the little children come to me, and do

---

ETERNITY

A. What conclusions concerning an afterlife have you reached?

B. Do you think it's possible to have a degree of certainty about where you will spend eternity?

C. Have you ever taken the time to explore what the Bible has to say concerning eternity?

A GOOD LIFE

A. Have you ever been able to get a handle on what you think your purpose in life is?

B. People say that money by itself cannot buy happiness; what does lead to a happy life?

C. Where do you feel you are really winning in life? losing at life?

BECOMING A CHRISTIAN

A. In your opinion, how does someone become a Christian?

B. Do you think it's possible to know God personally?

C. Has anyone ever shown you what the Bible says about how to begin a personal relationship with God?

not hinder them, for the kingdom of God belongs to such as these" (Mark 10:14). Jesus loves the way children ask innocent, wondering questions that make adults face uncomfortable truths. He wants all of his children to get in touch with the wide world of what we don't know and to tune in to that part of ourselves that is still fascinated with the people God made. Let's forget what the authority figures have told us and begin to wonder! It's attractive, it's liberating, and in its own way, it's irresistible.

REASONS FOR WONDER

There are four reasons active wondering questions work to open hearts wider for Jesus. To begin with, *wondering questions are nonthreatening*. In our cynical and defensive world, most people are on their guard against anything religious. They fear being taken in by sales pitches and schemes. They're skeptical of anyone who claims to have life-changing answers, but they will usually entertain caring and intelligent questions all day. Used properly, wondering questions change a listener into something far more than just a listener; wondering questions give listeners opportunities to become active *participants* in the conversation.

Wondering questions also remove barriers to evangelism because *they communicate humility*. Revealing that we're genuinely

WORLD EVENTS	GOOD VERSUS EVIL	BARRIERS TO BELIEF
A. How did 9/11 affect your view of God and the world?	A. Have you ever sensed the presence of evil?	A. What do you find the most difficult pill to swallow concerning belief in God?
B. When you watch or read the news, what conclusions do you draw about the nature of man?	B. Have you ever sensed the presence of God?	B. It's been said that Christians are like bulldogs: They have big teeth and a loud bark, but no brains. Have you found this stereotype to be true?
C. Is there a solution to social problems such as rape, murder, famine, war, racism, and divorce?	C. Have you had any major turning points in life?	C. Would it be fair to say that your disbelief in God is due more to your experience with Christians or with God himself?

wondering about lots of things demonstrates that we recognize we haven't got all the answers. Wondering questions let people know that we're actually interested in their thoughts and feelings, not just in hearing ourselves talk. The wondering attitude is anti-arrogant by nature. Perhaps that's why it's generally more popular to be searching for truth than to proclaim that you've found it. Wondering provides an innocent and natural way to engage in a two-way conversation about differing perceptions, worldviews, and ideas without ever arguing.

Most people don't believe an idea because it's true; they think it's true because *they* believe it. A third benefit of active wondering is that *it allows people to discover truth for themselves.* The insights we recognize on our own—even if we have help getting there—have far more power than anything we're told. Also, the intensity of conviction and commitment that comes from close personal scrutiny is far deeper than anything mere hearsay can produce. We've seen that the deeper and more personal the exploration, the more profound the resulting belief is likely to be.

Finally, good questions *cause others to begin asking their own good questions.* When people start earnestly looking for answers about life and God for themselves, they activate Christ's promise: "Ask and it will be given to you; seek and you will find; knock and the door will be opened to you" (Luke 11:9). All consistent seekers are starting on an irresistible journey toward God, even if they

---

RELATIVE TRUTH

A. It sounds like you value open-mindedness. Do you ever find yourself closing your mind to certain things, ideas, or people?

B. What criteria do you use when determining whether something is true or not?

C. Does your worldview allow for any absolutes?

MARRIAGE OR DATING

A. How did you meet your husband/wife (or boyfriend/girlfriend)?

B. What have you learned about yourself through marriage (or dating)?

C. What do you enjoy the most about marriage (or dating)? What do you enjoy the least?

LOVE

A. Has your understanding of the word *love* changed at all over the years?

B. Why do you think so many couples end up falling out of love?

C. If you could pass one secret on to the world about how to keep a relationship going and growing, what would it be?

don't realize it. Our job is simply to befriend and encourage them as they pursue their quest.

A good wondering question is intelligent and open, and it raises a point without being manipulative. But before you start peppering people with tons of questions, take time for silent wondering and listening to gain insight into some of the key categories below.

Backgrounds

- Where did they grow up?
- What was life like around their childhood homes?
- What things were most important to their families?
- Did they get in trouble a lot as children?
- What are their brothers and sisters like? How are they alike or different?
- Did they grow up going to church? Do they wish they had?

Tastes and opinions

- What subjects are they interested in?
- What causes are they passionate about?
- What kinds of shows do they allow or forbid their kids to watch on TV?
- What kinds of things bother or upset them?
- What do they think about cloning?
- Who are their favorite actors or actresses?

FINDING GOD

A. Why do you think so many people prefer to live as if God does not exist?

B. What would you want God to do to validate his existence and bring you to belief?

C. It's been said that many people never find God for the same reason a robber can't find the policeman standing on the corner. What does this saying mean to you?

RIGHT AND WRONG

A. Many have suggested that we are the product of a random evolution. If this is true, why do you think our culture still talks of right and wrong?

B. How do you teach your kids right from wrong?

C. What authority do you appeal to for such teaching in a world that says *right* and *wrong* have no meaning other than what we give the words?

DREAMS

A. What did you see yourself doing career-wise when you were eighteen?

B. What dreams have you let go of?

C. What dreams are you still hanging on to?

Thoughts and feelings

- What are their hearts' desires?
- If they had plenty of money and could do anything, what would they do?
- What are their priorities?
- What do they worry about?
- Who do they see as heroes and villains?
- Where does God fit into their pictures of the world?

Life directions

- Is there anything they're hungering for?
- What are the obstacles to their happiness?
- How satisfied are they with the state of their lives and relationships?
- What are their greatest challenges?
- Where are they currently in their relationships with God?
- How could you help them find more love, joy, and peace?

Once you've listened well and wondered silently for a while, you'll be ready to begin asking thoughtful and potentially life-changing questions that draw people toward God and pave the way for exciting things to come.

THE FUTURE

A. Are you optimistic or pessimistic about the future of our world?

B. Do you think it's easier or harder to raise kids in today's world?

C. What concerns you most as you think about your future?

MAJOR INFLUENCES

A. Who is the most impressive person you have ever met?

B. Has there been one book/movie that has greatly influenced you?

C. Besides your parents, is there any one person who stands out as having had a major influence in your life?

CHANGE

A. God has begun to change my life. Have you ever considered letting him change yours?

B. If God had his way with you, what do you think he would change first?

C. What scares you the most about letting God change your life?

Wonder Power

Has anyone ever asked you a question that changed the whole direction of your life?

Thirty years ago a humble Norwegian housewife started asking Steve questions that would lead him to faith in Jesus and shape his future. She was the devoted Christian mother of the family he lived with during his year as a foreign exchange student. From the very first, she made a huge impression on Steve. For starters, she stood nearly six feet tall and had hands large enough to palm a basketball. While tirelessly cooking and cleaning for a household of seven, she still focused lots of special time on Steve.

She didn't speak English, but she lived and talked in simple terms Steve could understand even with his limited Norwegian vocabulary. She made no secret of the fact that her life revolved around her commitment to Christ and her deep passion for the kingdom of God. The more skill Steve gained with the language, the more he enjoyed talking with her amid her seemingly constant housework. Their conversations often focused on Steve's curiosity about God and the Bible.

During one of these discussions, she posed a simple question that stopped him in his tracks. "Steve," she asked, "what do you think your life would look like if God got his way in your future?"

TAKING STOCK

A. What three principles have benefited you the most thus far in your life journey?

B. What, if anything, causes you to be hopeful about your future?

C. Is there anything left undone in your life that would cause you great sadness if you only had twenty-four hours to live?

GETTING TO KNOW YOU

A. As people get to know you, what do they enjoy most about you?

B. As people get to know you, what do they enjoy least?

C. As people get to know you, in what area do you feel most misunderstood?

LEADERSHIP

A. How would you describe your leadership style?

B. What leadership style do you respond best to?

C. Jesus was described as a servant leader. What kind of images does that stir up inside you?

Since Steve's heart had been well prepared through her many generous acts of kindness and her sacrificial willingness to listen, the question fell on fertile soil. She had poured out Christ's love, and it had awakened a craving for God in Steve's heart. As her simple, sincere question gave voice to the wondering of her soul, it focused all of their conversations on a single point. As Steve took it in, it crystallized his vague attraction to her faith into a palpable longing to know what his life *might* be like if he were to lay down his life for the God she served. It spun Steve on his heels and into a 180-degree change.

This question not only led Steve to give his heart to Jesus, but continues to change his life. Many years ago, it helped him turn away from a self-centered career path and toward ministry. To this day, God keeps bringing the question up. Now that Steve has stepped down from his role as the senior pastor of Vineyard Community Church, his new role as launching pastor is being driven by God's continual question, "What will the future look like if I get my way in your life, Steve?" Sometimes Steve wishes that the question could be answered just once so that things could be settled for good, but that isn't the way God works. He keeps asking his question again and again with new parameters and under new circumstances. Now that's a truly inspired question!

DIRECTION

A. Why do you do what you do?

B. What life experiences have molded you and motivated you to pursue this path?

C. Would you choose this same path again?

QUESTIONS FOR GOD

A. If you could ask God any three questions, what would they be?

B. What would you say if God asked this one question: "Are you for me or against me?"

C. How would you defend yourself if your response was put on trial?

SEX

A. Which sex do you think has the tougher path in life?

B. What do you enjoy most about the opposite sex?

C. What do you enjoy most about being male/female?

WONDERING QUESTIONS

Doug has become a connoisseur of wondering questions. He says great questions rarely have simple answers. They plant seeds that grow into intriguing dialogue. Doug explains:

Great questions start where people are, not where we would like them to be. As the writer said in Proverbs 20:5, "The purposes of a man's heart are deep waters, but a man of understanding draws them out." If the body of Christ wants to succeed in reaching today's world, we need to learn to ask higher quality questions. Christians have already proven that we enjoy giving answers; unfortunately, we are too often answering questions nobody is asking. Outstanding questions stimulate great thoughts. They also serve as a kind of spiritual stethoscope to help us hear the sounds of hidden spiritual struggles within another's heart.

In the last half of the twentieth century, D. James Kennedy raised two great questions that have helped many thousands to share the gospel.

1. Have you come to a place in your spiritual life where you can say you know for certain that if you were to die today you would go to heaven?

2. Suppose that you were to die today and stand before God and that he were to ask you, "Why should I let you into my heaven?" What would you say?

HATE	DEATH	CONTROL
A. Have you ever hated anyone?	A. If you could choose the manner of your death, how would you like to go?	A. It's been said that life is largely out of our control. If that's true, why do so many people try to control the life they live?
B. Has anyone ever hated you?	B. What would you like written on your tombstone or spoken at your funeral?	B. Do you struggle with that?
C. Do you think there is a solution for this emotion?	C. Does the thought of death scare you?	C. What kinds of things do you think can be controlled in life?

Unfortunately as our culture drifts further from God and the Bible, fewer and fewer people relate well to questions that assume a belief in heaven and hell. Many don't believe in an afterlife, or if they do, they embrace a vague belief in some form of reincarnation. Questions that we once opened with have become more and more premature. Like impatient doctors, evangelists are not listening to people's hearts well enough to understand what is really going on. Our good intentions often have arrogant undertones that subtly declare, "I know what's wrong with you…just listen to me while I prescribe your cure." This assumption belittles the people we're trying to reach and presumes that we know how to run their lives better than they do.

Wondering questions help us move from the land of monologue to the land of dialogue—while there is still some chance someone might actually be listening. Depending on your spiritual background, this journey could be more difficult than you think. Take a look at how truth is dispensed in most churches, and you'll realize that monologue is our model of choice. Each week many pastors spend up to twenty-five hours perfecting a twenty- to forty-minute monologue for Sunday morning. Once the sermon is over, there's rarely any opportunity for questions. Apart from the remote possibility that someone might schedule an appointment with the preacher to ask questions, it's all monologue.

HABITS

A. What kinds of habits do you struggle with most?

B. Do you ever find yourself wondering why you don't do the things you want to do and end up doing the things you don't want to do?

C. Do you think there is anything out there that can set you free from this cycle?

CHILDHOOD

A. How would you change the way you were raised?

B. What things are you going to do or are you doing as you raise your kids?

C. What values from your childhood do you want to pass on to your kids?

QUESTIONS FOR JESUS

A. If Jesus were here right now, what would you ask him for?

B. How do you think he would answer?

C. How would you feel if that happened?

The model rule states, "You will do unto others what has been modeled unto you." So when most people start talking to not-yet-Christians about their faith, what they say naturally comes in the form of a sermon. As Doug says, "We go all *monological* on them." He suggests trying a forty-day fast from any kind of monologue. In case you feel withdrawal symptoms coming on, we're going to give you something to help you kick your habit. We want you to learn how to be "dialogical" (not diabolical), instead.

Questions That Don't Work

Irresistible evangelists learn to avoid some types of questions. For instance, it's smart to avoid "soapbox" questions. These aren't really questions at all; they're rhetorical challenges that demonstrate that you really don't care what the person is going to say. They're convenient springboards from which you can launch into a monologue designed to set people straight. Common soapbox questions might be "What do you think about Jesus? Do you need forgiveness?" or "Are you saved?"

We often spring other questions designed to set a rhetorical trap later in the conversation. Here's an example: "Is there anything more important to you than your family's safety?" Slick car

---

The goal of wondering questions is always to open a dialogue in which you learn about others and they learn about you. The questions aren't a springboard for a gospel presentation, they're a springboard for getting to know someone on a deeper level. Don't worry if the questions that come to your mind don't sound particularly spiritual. And don't worry if they are. As long as you aren't insensitive or trying to push toward a conclusion, most questions will open the door to wonder.

salesmen use such scripted, entrapment questions all the time. It's a clever way to set up a case for why you should buy a Volvo. The idea is to get people saying yes to a series of questions and then to spring the trap and hopefully close the sale. A common *resistible* evangelism example might be "People say that money doesn't buy happiness. Would you agree?" or "Do you care whether your children go to heaven?" This technique may work for people selling cars or pitching time shares in Florida, but it's just not kosher in evangelism.

The goal is not to sell anyone anything.

We'll say it again: The goal is not to sell anyone anything. It is not even to try to convince anyone of the truth of an idea. The goal is to encourage people to start looking and moving in God's direction.

ONE MORE SPORTS ANALOGY

If you're a tennis fan, it's exhilarating to watch two good players volley the ball back and forth. Each tries to gain advantage by drawing the other out of position and then hitting a decisive shot, called a winner, to score a point. Unfortunately, many good-intentioned believers view evangelistic dialogue as the same kind of game. They view the person they're talking with as an opponent. Every time they score a point, they think the other person is one step closer to conceding the game. Zeal prompts many of us to try to win with an overpowering serve. If that doesn't do it, we continue to pepper our opponents with volley after volley of surefire "winners," even though our opponents actually walked off the court the moment the contest began. In other cases, our opponents stay on the court and dig in to send a few forceful volleys of their own back at the Christian who is taking potshots at their worldview. With this approach, everyone loses.

We're far better off learning to hit gentle serves by asking good, caring questions. If the ball is returned, our goal should be to see how long we can keep it in play by listening and perhaps posing a few more good questions. Should our dialogue partners quit hitting the ball back into our court, maybe it's time to stop playing for the moment. Like most tennis players, they'll probably look forward to another friendly game sometime in the future. At some point in our evangelistic dialogue, our hope is to lower the net altogether and join our partners (not opponents) as they begin to pursue answers to the big questions of their lives.

WONDER BEGETS WONDER

Ask great questions, but don't set yourself up to answer them. A good evangelistic wonderer's goal is to open honest dialogue that ignites imagination and leads participants to consider new ideas and ways of thinking. Wondering stretches Christians to fearlessly embrace and test our own beliefs while acknowledging and reinforcing reasonable conclusions of not-yet-Christians. Since we want to beget spiritual wondering in others, we must be ready to discuss (not debate) the issues and questions that are really on their minds. If we want others to stretch themselves to honestly consider questions about God, we must be willing to do the same and consider any questions they might raise. It even becomes *fun* if we can give up the idea that we're trying to win a tug of war. Since we don't pretend to have all the answers, the only surefire way to fail in active wondering is by being either dishonest or disrespectful.

The only surefire way to fail in active wondering is by being either dishonest or disrespectful.

Most active wondering begins when we connect with someone about an area of interest or need, and it happens naturally when we look for ways to serve and listen to people. It's exactly what happened with Doug's friend Annette. Over the years, she had befriended a sweet, older lady who lived next door. This devout Christian woman lived alone until her adult son moved in. He was an MIT grad student who returned home after a messy divorce. Even after he moved in, Annette continued checking in on his elderly mother. Soon she had befriended him, as well.

When the son asked why she was being so helpful to him and his mother, Annette told him that she was just trying to show God's love in practical ways. At the mention of her faith in Christ, he said he was glad for her but that he had grown up and moved past all of that. He went on to tell her that he was writing a book on philosophy. Annette sensed that God was calling her to continue reaching out to him, but she was stumped about how to do it.

"The last thing I wanted was to dig out all my Josh McDowell and Hugh Ross books on apologetics," Annette recalled. "I'm just not good at arguing with people—especially not an MIT graduate who's writing a book on philosophy! I was so relieved when I talked to Doug and he suggested active wondering!"

Doug suggested that Annette begin asking some questions about their common interest in his mother. He recommended that she

- keep on building the relationship,
- talk to him about what he likes to talk about,
- wonder aloud about how his mother's faith affects him,
- ask what his book is about,
- listen to his spiritual questions, and
- try to discern what his spiritual address might be.

These kinds of topics will naturally open a dialogue in which you can wonder back and forth about lots of things. People who feel safe talking with you will often be willing to zero in on directional and, eventually, spiritual questions.

If this doesn't sound very systematic, that's because people and relationships are all very different. But that doesn't mean we have no purpose or direction. Wondering does involve some *wandering*, but there is a natural flow that leads us in a God-ward direction. We initiate dialogue by entering another person's world and trying to accurately understand that person's perspective. We want to learn about and from the person. We want to get to know the person inside. As the relationship becomes friendly and mutual, it's natural to begin exploring biblical principles without ever arguing or citing chapter and verse. If we move at a comfortable pace and resist getting hooked into making speeches, wonderful things can happen. If we wonder well, we'll have multiple opportunities for conversations on multiple issues.

AWAKENING OTHERS' WONDER

You may remember the story of how folk singer and rock icon Bob Dylan began wondering about the Christian faith. Steve has the inside story from the people who were actually involved. It began when some musicians who were touring with Bob (and who happened to be Christians) began having wondering conversations with him about what was happening in his life. For decades he had been a poet and a searcher after truth, but lately it seemed all his friends were asking him the same question: What are you looking for?

Dylan began thinking seriously about the ultimate direction and expressions of life. He had talked to lots of people about lots of answers, but he kept landing on the same spot again and again. He was fascinated by the life of Jesus. He was also intrigued by fellow musicians who went to the Vineyard Church in Los Angeles and who seemed to be faithfully following Christ. He began to ask them questions—lots and lots of questions. Then Dylan invited pastors from that church to come to his house. They stayed up until all hours of the morning talking about Jesus and God. And it was exhilarating! Dylan was close to coming to Christ—and *he* was asking all the questions.

When Bob Dylan publicly professed his faith in Jesus, many of his longtime fans didn't understand. How could the ultimate rebel become a born-again Christian? But that's when conservative Christians began pressuring him to say and do things he didn't believe in. It seemed like everyone wanted him to be someone he really wasn't. When he announced that he was returning to his

Jewish roots, his fans breathed a sigh of relief, and the religious firestorm died down.

Steve isn't giving away any secrets when he says that Dylan hasn't abandoned his faith in Jesus. Like many other famous people, he's just a lot quieter and much more selective about who he talks to about it. You won't hear any Christian buzzwords in the lyrics of his recent songs, but you might perceive the sound of a soul attuned to a God-ward journey.

Whatever you believe about Bob, the lesson here is a good one. If we want to bring people to Jesus, we must not pressure them to conform to our image of what they should be. Wondering encourages people to think for themselves and to be who they really are. The goal is not to get people to agree to a set of doctrinal propositions or meet minimum requirements for membership in our Christian club. The goal isn't to get them to stop smoking or swearing. It's to help them move closer and closer to initiating a one-to-one relationship with God. Wondering done well always expresses God's grace and openhearted, just-as-you-are acceptance.

If we want to bring people to Jesus, we must not pressure them to conform to our image of what they should be.

When was the last time a pre-Christian started peppering you with spiritual questions? When people begin to question us, it's a sure sign they're ready for us to share the how-to part of the gospel. After coming progressively closer and closer, they've arrived on the green. That's what Chapter 9 is all about.

Active
SHARING

> "One of the most exciting
> spiritual adventures in life
> is helping another human being
> find God."
>
> —JOHN ORTBERG,
> *If You Want to Walk on Water,*
> *You've Got to Get Out of the Boat*

> "We loved you so much that we
> were delighted to share with
> you not only the gospel of God
> but our lives as well."
>
> —1 THESSALONIANS 2:8

In every serious relationship, people begin at some point to consider making a lifelong commitment. The feelings that come into play in thinking about that commitment, as expressed in this imaginary Dear Abby letter, are much the same as the feelings involved in contemplating a committed relationship with Jesus:

Dear Abby,

I need your advice desperately. I think I'm falling for a wonderful guy, and I'm not sure what to do. I've been attracted to him ever since a friend introduced us. I've been seeing him for some time now, and our relationship is progressing to where I'm getting a little scared. It feels like this might be the "real thing" I've been looking for all my life. He's made it clear that he loves me, and I think I might like being with him forever. My big question to you, Abby, is "How do I know the right time to commit?" Please give me some wisdom. My friends aren't much help, and my mom just wants grandchildren!

Cold Feet in Kansas

Dear Cold Feet,

Thanks for sharing your heart so honestly. I can't think of anyone who's considered marriage who hasn't had some fear of commitment— at least not anyone who was paying attention! The fact that you're seriously wrestling with the concept of commitment is evidence that you're taking this relationship seriously and that it means something to you. If it helps, this is one of the most common topics of letters I receive. I say, if you love him, take all the time you need to make sure he's who he says he is—then take the risk and go for it. The eternal love of your life only comes by once in a lifetime.

Abby

The closest emotional parallel to making a faith commitment to Christ is saying, "I do!" in marriage vows. After all, Scripture calls the church the bride of Christ. We can spend months of nervous preparation and planning to design the perfect setting in which to utter our lifelong promises to each other. Then time-honored, ceremonial words solemnize the commitment. The more traditional the background we come from—or in the case of helping folks come to know Christ, the more classic the evangelistic approach we subscribe to—the more emphasis we are likely to place on the words uttered in that special moment.

Many approaches teach us to focus our evangelistic efforts on getting people to say, "I do!" to Jesus but forget about what comes before and what comes after. Just as a good marriage requires much more than an impressive wedding, irresistible evangelism involves a great deal more than just getting someone to pray a prayer. Vows are wonderful for people who are standing on the brink, ready to make the plunge into a lifelong commitment. Praying to express trust in Christ is very important, but it's still just one of the hundreds of steps (before and after) on our journey toward intimacy with God.

Irresistible evangelism involves a great deal more than just getting someone to pray a prayer.

Many Christians talk about developing an intimate *personal relationship* with God, but the message they present to not-yet-Christians focuses almost exclusively on explaining how the atoning death of Jesus satisfies the requirements of God's justice. This is a little bit like trying to induce a prospective bride to get married because she will gain legal claim to all of her husband's possessions. From this point of view, the plan of salvation sounds much more like an impersonal legal arrangement than a loving relationship. Talking about doctrines such as justification by faith and atonement by the substitutionary death of Jesus is usually unnecessarily confusing. The doctrines may accurately explain what happens (in a legal sense) when we pray to accept Jesus, but they don't paint a very relational picture. In some ears, the plan of salvation even sounds like the spiritual equivalent of arranging a marriage of convenience to fool the Immigration and Naturalization Service into granting citizenship.

Most soon-to-be brides and grooms are much more interested in love, trust, friendship, tenderness, partnership, and passion than in calculating the material benefits that may come with marriage. Relationship is the true heart of the matter. It's the same for not-yet-Christians. They need to see, hear, feel, taste, and touch convincing evidence that Jesus offers the kind of relationship they've been longing for. Following Jesus is much more than just a handy way to gain admittance to heaven or to avoid hell. It's more than a magic formula for salvation. It is *at least* as real and dynamic a relationship as marriage is.

Like the process of finding a mate, building a relationship with Jesus involves more than one big decision. It takes lots of tiny experiences that build a foundation of trust and inspire people to hope that perhaps the God of the universe may cherish them and care about their individual feelings, hopes, and dreams.

In the Western world, committed love relationships usually follow a natural pattern. First we gradually "fall in interest." Then we "fall in like" and then "in love." Eventually, we commit. Deep relationship grows as we fall into a lifetime rhythm of mutual giving and receiving.

We've seen this natural process again and again as we observe those who have managed to build healthy and loving marriages. Even though the best marriages we've seen are still imperfect, the Bible consistently uses matrimony to illustrate how a fulfilling relationship with God grows.

One example of the progression from interest to like to love is illustrated in the path Doug and Martha took to marriage.

The Perfect Fit

When Doug was on a ministry trip in Poland many years ago (before the fall of the Communist government), he passed a fur market that sold top-quality fur coats for fifty to one-hundred dollars. On a wild impulse, he bought a beautiful women's fur coat and decided to start praying to God to fill it with a beautiful woman (to be his wife). He tells the story:

When I came home from my trip, some of my friends found out about the coat, and it became a running joke between us. Months later I started dating a very nice girl, and—without telling me—a buddy shared the coat story with her. When she found out where I kept it, she crept in and tried it on. She was really mad that it didn't fit. Maybe that relationship was doomed. Time passed, and I kept praying God would bring me the right woman. I didn't mind helping him out in the search; I put legs on my prayers by asking plenty of women out. Then I met Martha at a party.

Falling in Interest

She was with a large group of women, but something about her caught my eye. I went over and talked with her for a while and really enjoyed the conversation. Somehow though, she slipped away. A few minutes later, I saw her leaving the party with her friends. I didn't see her for a long time after that, but I kept thinking, That's the kind of woman I'm looking for.

Nearly a year after that first meeting, Martha came to a singles group that Doug frequented.

I saw that she was leaving. I rushed out to talk to her before she could get away—and she nearly ran me over with her car on the way out! Later that night, we ran into each other at a restaurant and I asked if she remembered me. To my shock and dismay, she had no memory of me whatsoever! This time I wasn't going to let her get away without first getting her phone number.

Falling in Like

After a few phone conversations, they made a date. Doug boldly invited Martha to visit his hometown to meet his family one weekend—and, remarkably, she accepted. Doug had borrowed his dad's old grain truck to do some hauling, and it was the only transportation available.

Our date started awkwardly when I realized she needed help just climbing up into the front seat. It was a loud, teeth-rattling, four-hour drive to my folks' house. The little conversation we had on the way was shouted over the deafening roar and clatter of the old truck. It was a good thing I had decided to allow Martha to witness what my life was really like so she could see what she might be getting into. That night we went to a demolition derby (seriously, we really did!), and the next morning I was scheduled to preach at my parents' church. Not only did Martha come along, she stood in the receiving line with me after the sermon and greeted everyone on the way out. All the older church ladies had kind of adopted me and had been praying for me to find a godly wife. When they saw Martha, they made a big fuss, telling her what a great catch I was and how happy they were that I had finally found a nice girl like her. It was our first date, but they were sure it was meant to be.

We survived that date and continued seeing each other for several months.

Falling in Love

As their relationship deepened, Martha confessed to Doug that he didn't fit the picture she had in her mind of a potential husband. She had been praying that God would send her someone like her father, an accomplished Christian businessman, not a Campus Crusade staff member who had to raise his own salary. But there was something special about Doug that had reached her heart. He had fallen for her practically at first sight, but it took time for her to realize that he was the man she really wanted. Doug's story continues:

The night I proposed was my birthday. I had secretly told her family what I planned to do, and they helped set the scene. Their job was to talk Martha into taking me out to a specific restaurant where I had secretly bribed the management to play our favorite song—the theme from Somewhere in Time—*over the sound system when I was ready to propose and to hang the special fur coat I had bought all those years before in a closet nearby. I hadn't told the coat story to Martha, because I had no idea if it would fit her. But whether it fit or not, I knew she was the one.*

Commitment

As we got ready to go, Martha said, "Why don't we go to Red Lobster?" That was not the right restaurant! I tried not to choke and dodged the bullet by insisting that, since it was my birthday, I should pick the restaurant. The whole restaurant staff knew what was going on, and all through dinner they treated us both like royalty. When we finished eating, she gave me my birthday present, and I opened it. Then I stood up and, in a disappointed voice, said, "I was hoping for something more for my birthday...would you marry me?" When she said yes, I slipped the ring on her finger and told her to close her eyes. I got the coat and told her its special story. She tried it on—and it was a perfect fit!

Martha still wears the coat on special occasions, and her mother loves to tell me that it's a miracle that it fit. Martha is petite and needs a longer than usual sleeve length so that it is nearly impossible to buy her clothes.

PREPARED TO SHARE

The hidden matchmaker in all of us responds to romantic stories like Doug and Martha's, but most of us don't associate any romance with sharing Jesus. Even people who relish the idea of setting up their single friends with blind dates still tend to see evangelism as a daunting and unpleasant duty. It's actually much more fun than human matchmaking—and you know without a doubt that, whoever it is you're matching up with him, Jesus is the perfect fit! Not only that, but you can be sure the Holy Spirit has already been working his magic too.

> Evangelism is actually much more fun than human matchmaking.

The nineteenth-century Scottish writer George MacDonald pictured our part and God's part in the process by saying, "The work is his, but we must take our willing share. When the blossom breaks forth, the more it is ours, the more it is his."[1] We have an exciting and critical part to play in opening hearts to Jesus, and like Paul we can take a reasonable share of parental pride when those we share with come to new birth.[2]

When we prepare to share, it's also important to consider our own relationship with the person we hope to connect with. People will relate quite differently to us depending on whether they perceive us as strangers, acquaintances, friends, or eternal brothers or sisters. The opportunities and challenges each of these relationships presents revolve around how *safe* people feel about opening up to us. That's why Dave uses the acrostic SAFE to help people remember the pluses and minuses associated with each.

Perfect Strangers

S stands for strangers. In childhood most of us were taught not to talk to strangers. Of course, if we followed this advice, we would never meet anyone outside our immediate families. We meet and interact with strangers all the time. However, when we encounter someone we don't know, we tend to be at least a little bit guarded. Without consciously thinking about it, we check the other person out. Based on clothing, grooming, facial expressions, posture, and general looks, we intuitively decide how far to trust the person. If people look friendly, they may be safe to talk to; if they look unattractive or scary, we'll probably avoid them.

A warm smile and a welcoming look can diminish natural distrust, but they will not eliminate it. Strangers have to prove themselves trustworthy by being kind and considerate and by showing respect for other people's boundaries. Kindness outreaches provide a great way to initiate short encounters with strangers that can build trust. Most will receive our small gifts and acts of kindness with gratitude and continue quickly on their way, but some will stop and have a conversation.

Steve Bowen, a pastor in Dayton, Ohio, explains how he responds to the why and what questions his teams get.

"Many times they ask questions like 'Why are you doing this?' or 'What kind of church would wash my car for free?' Our response to the why question is to smile and reply, 'We're doing it to show you God's love in a practical way.'

"We answer the what question by saying, 'The kind of church that washes cars for free.' "

One of Steve's hopes is that lots of strangers will experience lots of kind touches from lots of kind Christians over time.

Fiona pulled up for a free car wash. I greeted her with a smile and handed her a small packet with three pieces of bubble gum and a connection card. I said "Hi! I'm Steve, and here is some bubble gum you can chew while we wash your car."

She replied, "What's the deal? You guys gave me a soft drink at a stoplight. You came to my door with a free light bulb. Now you're washing my car for free? What's up?"

I said, "What's up is that Jesus is in love with you, and we want to show you his love in a practical way!" Her positive yet puzzled look showed me she was interested, so I continued, "You ought to come check us out sometime."

She paused, smiled, and shrugged in a noncommittal way. It was obvious she was interested, but the mention of church was a bit of a turnoff. I switched gears and backed off a little, knowing that God was still working on her. As she drove away, I shouted, "Have a great day, and thanks for letting us wash your car!"

Steve's encounter was typical. Building interest and trust with a stranger often takes lots of little touches. Even though Fiona was cool toward the idea of coming to church, she was starting to "fall in interest" with Jesus. You don't need an organized project to give lots of small touches. Simple things like offering to help someone carry a heavy bag or giving someone a free newspaper at the airport can open natural opportunities for sharing. If strangers ask why you're being kind, just tell them you think it's what Jesus would do. With strangers the important thing is to keep your sharing brief, simple, and nonthreatening. Make it clear you aren't trying to get them to do or agree to anything.

Sometimes strangers feel safer talking to someone they're unlikely to ever see again. You've probably struck up a conversation with a perfect stranger on an airplane and heard the person open up about his or her dreams and struggles. It's amazing how many evangelistic conversations all three of us have had with the people sitting next to us on airplanes. The reason is that none of us is shy about talking very simply about what we really care about—and what we really care about is God's love. Dave says sometimes he has evangelistic conversations even when he doesn't want to. One instance sticks out in his mind:

I was flying back from Scandinavia after leading a conference there. I got to my seat and noticed an elderly handicapped woman sitting in it. I was a little upset because, whenever I take transatlantic flights, I take pains to reserve an aisle seat next to the bulkhead so I can stretch out my legs and sleep. The flight attendant was very apologetic, but the bottom line was that she had given away my seat.

The plane was packed, and there was no room in first class. She offered me a bottle of champagne and her sincere apologies, but I was still ticked—especially when she seated me in the last seat available. It was in the center, between a family with three children (the youngest a crying infant) and the most extroverted and unmistakably inebriated Swedish businessman I had ever met.

I was angry, exhausted, and anticipating eight hours of nerve-jangling torment at twenty-thousand feet when the drunken Swedish man asked me what I'd been doing in Scandinavia. I briefly told him that I'd been leading a conference for church leaders and that I was very tired and hoped he would excuse me if I wasn't very sociable.

For the next seven and a half hours, he told me his life's story, pausing regularly to call the flight attendant to refill his whiskey glass. Although I pretended to read and sleep and tried many times to end the conversation, he persisted. When I finally gave in and talked to him, he was discoursing about religion and God. He asked what I believed, and I reluctantly said that I believed that God cared for and even delighted in him personally. This shut him up for nearly a full minute. Then he turned and soberly confessed a sin he had committed when he was a teenager. Slowly and in a remarkably clear voice, he admitted, "Ever since then, I've known that I was on my way to hell."

Even though he was a perfect stranger—and a pretty annoying one at that moment—I told him that there was nothing the Jesus I knew couldn't forgive him for. As I told him briefly about my own experience with forgiveness, he became very serious and uncharacteristically quiet.

Suddenly the fasten-your-seat-belt warning pinged, followed by the announcement to the cabin crew to prepare for landing. Between helping to find children's toys under the seat and getting rid of all the empty glasses, we didn't get to finish our conversation. Soon I was rushing from the plane to catch the shuttle bus and connect to my next flight. The Swedish man got on behind me, put his hand on my shoulder, and said—to my everlasting embarrassment—"No Christian has ever been so friendly to me. I want to know your kind of God."

What really happened in that man's heart is impossible to say, but to Dave it seemed that the Holy Spirit amplified what little patience and caring he'd expressed and used it to draw the man's heart a little closer to Jesus. As we've said, that's the irresistible evangelism goal.

GREAT ACQUAINTANCES

A stands for acquaintances. You probably have hundreds of them without realizing it. You know their faces and maybe their names, and you probably share at least a few things in common with them. You may live on the same street or work in the same office. An acquaintance may be your lawyer, your hairdresser, or your mailman. You barely know acquaintances, but the exciting thing is that they're known and loved by your God. Each is a brother or sister waiting to happen.

Barb wasn't looking for God, but she found him when she was looking for a babysitter. She was an atheist who'd been raised in a Jewish household. She'd just settled into a successful career as a private-practice therapist when she discovered she was expecting a child. A difficult pregnancy forced her to cut back on clients, and when the baby came, her life turned upside down.

 We were suddenly broke, and the baby was sick all the time, so I had to cut back my caseload again. After months of sleepless

nights filled with worry and despair, I decided to hire a babysitter for my son so I could work at least half time. When I finally located Robin, or Bin-Bin as my son later called her, little did I know she would become my spiritual mentor and guide.

Bin-Bin is everything I'm not. She is quiet, self-effacing, humble, and intensely shy. Normally I wouldn't have paid much attention to her, but during my son's first year, she became very important in my life. On many occasions, she would drive all the way across town to drop off a prescription for me or just to provide a few quiet words of comfort. After months of benefiting from her quiet kindness, I finally asked her why she was so different. She told me it was Jesus, and for the first time in my life, I really listened.

I'd always been taught to distrust Christians because they're the ones who had hated, persecuted, and systematically slaughtered millions of Jews. When I was five or six, I remember being shown black and white footage of concentration camp victims being piled into gas ovens. I'll never forget seeing the skeletal bodies of children, many around my age at the time, being heaped into a gigantic pile with a pitchfork. We were told that these were Jewish children, and the same fate could happen to us someday if we forgot our heritage. Two messages stuck in my mind: First, that Jews are a persecuted people who must stick together at all costs. Second, non-Jews are never to be trusted.

Bin-Bin was different from anyone I'd ever met, Christian or Jew. I wanted to discover more about what made her so special, so I started attending her church. For several months, my husband and I met with the pastor. I knew the events of my life were converging toward a single moment. I finally surrendered my heart to Bin-Bin's Jesus. I had spent years speaking to large audiences about how to transform lives with therapy—now I just want to learn how to reach out quietly, gently, and unobtrusively for God's glory, just like Bin-Bin!

Barb didn't know that hiring Robin as a babysitter would change her life. Lots of Christians (including her own husband) had tried and failed to reach her with Christ's good news. They had talked about heaven and hell and argued about ideas—without success. But

Robin just did her best to love and serve Barb from an insignificant acquaintance into a beloved friend. She did it quietly and without ever raising her voice. Everything about her said, "I really care about you!" Robin's actions led to questions, the questions led to answers, and the simple answers she shared led to choices. Robin's life is a great example of how genuine loving turns acquaintances into real friends and helps them fall in love with Jesus.

Genuine loving turns acquaintances into real friends and helps them fall in love with Jesus.

FRIENDS AND FAMILY

F stands for friends and family. These are the most influential people in our lives. People will buy an expensive car or a computer because a friend says he or she likes it. They'll check out a church because a family member says it's a good place. Many studies cite the influence of a friend or family member as the number one reason Christians give for making their initial decision to follow Christ. All this being said, sharing Jesus with those close to us is often surprisingly tough. We love them and want the best for them, but it's hard to overcome the challenges of familiarity.

We can't get away with *pretending* that we've got our acts together with these folks. They're close enough to us to see us as we are and to catalog effortlessly all our flaws and shortcomings. Since they often delight in pointing out any hypocrisy in our lives, the big challenge is to be painstakingly honest in admitting our weaknesses and bad habits while loving and serving them in the best ways we can.

With close friends and family members, *explanation* of faith is typically much more powerful if it is preceded by lots of *demonstration*. Perhaps that's why in 1 Peter 2:12 the apostle tells us to live such good lives among those who don't yet believe that, though they may accuse us of wrongdoing, they will see our good deeds and glorify

God. We can expect our motives and actions to be questioned; even so, we need to keep up the kindness! Anyone who's tried this will probably agree that showing faith in loving actions is more effective in drawing people toward Christ than lectures or heated arguments.

On this front, few things are more spiritually attractive than self-effacing honesty. When we talk about our family life or marriage with our friends, we needn't sugar coat it. We mustn't pretend to live like Ozzy and Harriet Nelson when our reality is more like Ozzy and Sharon Osbourne's. Being real and staying real is incredibly freeing. And nothing is more appealing than true honesty and freedom in Christ. If the people we love catch even a little glimpse of what genuine freedom looks like, they'll be irresistibly drawn to find it for themselves.

The world is longing to see the openness, friendliness, and joy that people who are truly free radiate. It's been said, "All the world asks of Christians is that they really be Christians." In 1 Corinthians 7:12-16, the Apostle Paul encourages those who are married to unbelieving spouses not to leave but to do what they can to contribute to their mates' salvation. Countless spouses have heeded this call and seen that their actions really do speak louder than words.

All the world asks of Christians is that they really be Christians.

Dave has taught marriage seminars for many years. In one seminar, he regularly asks husbands and wives to complete the sentence "I really feel loved when..."

You'd be amazed at how small and seemingly insignificant the actions are on that list. It includes things like speaking a kind word or taking a minute to ask how the day went and then really listening without interrupting. Spouses felt loved when they got telephone calls or received notes with handwritten words of endearment. Being considerate and doing small chores, such as washing the dishes or vacuuming the car without being asked, also went a long way.

When husbands and wives (or children or friends) truly feel loved, it's amazing how open they will become to hearing about the things we care about. When our mouths speak about God's love and about Jesus in the midst of daily acts of thoughtfulness, it's amazing how much credibility is added to our words.

After demonstrating Christ's love and putting his truth into lots of small actions, explaining faith to the people we care about becomes much easier. Christlike actions naturally lead to personal explanations. People ask, "Why did you do that?" and "What's so different about you?" When questions like these start to arise, thank the person for noticing and be ready to answer in brief, honest ways that explain why your relationship with Jesus has been changing how you think and act.

When you honestly explain how God is helping you with your struggles, most people's curiosity will be aroused, and they will ask more wondering questions. If not, you can use active listening and wondering questions of your own to focus on them: "It sounds like you're curious about spiritual things. Have you had similar experiences?" or "I know you aren't into religion, but you sound like you're kind of attracted to what I've been saying about Jesus. What do you think about him?"

Be honest and loving. Forget all your clever arguments.

Be ready for long dialogues with lots of questions and concerns. Be calm and trust that God is working. Be honest and loving. Forget all your clever arguments. When your caring actions and calm sharing combine with the work of the Holy Spirit, you'll see people start falling in love with Jesus. Once that happens, a desire for commitment naturally follows.

Again, don't rush it. As someone once said, Christ's salvation is a free gift; it just costs us everything. Christ gives his love and life to us for free, but as in any good marriage, we need to freely give our hearts and our lives to him in return. *There is a cost to commitment that honesty won't allow us to gloss over.* Moving from being single into a loving and committed marriage changes our lives in ways we never imagined; giving our hearts to Jesus is the spiritual equivalent. Encouraging people to count the cost of committing their hearts to Jesus won't "blow the deal" any more than it does in considering marriage. It is just good sense to help folks explore what their future with Jesus might look like.

Lots of good tools exist for helping people understand and make a clear commitment to Christ once they are ready.[3] Such tools generally include a simple scriptural explanation of what happens in heaven when we speak words of commitment to Jesus here on earth. Almost all of these tools work well if we use them at the right time and in the right way. John 1:12 tells us, "To all who received him, to those who believed in his name, he gave the right to become children of God." There's no magic formula here. The "Christ, come into my heart" prayer most of us have been taught is never actually modeled in the Bible, but the Spirit of that prayer is on every page of the Old and New Testaments.

Think of a prayer of commitment as a marriage vow.

In the Bible, people coming into God's presence seem to intuitively know the right thing to say. Isaiah, Moses, Daniel, and Peter all prayed something like, "Here I am, God," then automatically acknowledged their powerlessness and brokenness before him. The presence of God reveals our best intentions and efforts as pitifully insufficient. We want to answer his call, but we're unable. That's where Jesus steps in. As Romans 10:11 says, "Anyone who trusts in him will never be put to shame." Instead, "Everyone who calls on the name of the Lord will be saved" (verse 13).

It helps to think of a prayer of commitment as a marriage vow. A good commitment prayer spells out what people are actually committing to. It's like the "in sickness and health, for richer and poorer" part of a wedding ceremony. Those ancient words say things that are vitally important and need to be said.

Years ago some friends of Dave's got married on the beach in California. They wrote their own vows, and it wasn't too difficult to predict that the marriage would be short-lived when they promised to stay together "…as long as we both shall love." This weak promise pretty much guaranteed that as soon as trouble hit and *feelings* of love faded, the marriage relationship would be over.

The basic commitment prayer we like to use is short and sweet: "Jesus, here I am. Thank you for loving me. I receive you now as my Savior and Lord for now and for eternity. Forgive my sins, take control of my life, and make me the kind of person you want me to be."

ETERNAL FRIENDS AND FAMILY

E is for eternal brother or sister. As we said earlier, we believe that evangelism and discipleship are part of the same process of continually moving people closer to God. Sharing our faith doesn't stop when strangers, acquaintances, and friends commit their lives to Christ. The process of sharing takes on a new importance as we try to help the newly committed person learn the ropes of the new relationship. We do this primarily by sensitive self-disclosure. It's a bit like an older married lady coming alongside a new bride to help her learn about setting up housekeeping.

A committed relationship with Jesus opens up a whole new world where developing good habits early can have long-term positive outcomes. Learning the ropes of prayer, getting into the Bible, and getting involved with a community of others who are actively seeking to follow Christ are all essential for long-term spiritual growth. It is also at this early stage of faith that many people are incredibly effective and enthusiastic in sharing with others. Every church needs lots of these spiritual newlyweds reminding us of our first love and challenging us to keep it real.

When Justin, a young physician who recently committed his life to Jesus, joined Dave's small group, he revolutionized it. His questions about prayer were fresh and thought-provoking. His early, honest struggles in his marriage and with how to follow and obey Jesus in everyday situations were relevant to everyone in the group. We all benefited from his passion and curiosity, and he benefited from having friends ready to listen, offer support, and give him guidance when he needed it. Spiritual newlyweds and "oldlyweds" desperately need each other if we want to go higher up and deeper into our walk with Jesus. The fresh breath of the Spirit won't touch us when we play it safe. We all need to get out of what's comfortable and begin actively sharing the richness of relationship with God.

Following the SAFE acrostic is an adventurous way of getting and staying healthy as a community of Christ-lovers and Jesus-followers. The resistible religion of the city of man and the lifeless evangelism that flows from it won't lead to many happy, lasting spiritual unions. But joining with the irresistible love of God will invariably lead to a tenfold, a hundredfold, even a thousandfold population explosion. We've laid out the principles of serving, listening, wondering, and sharing; now the fun begins.

KINDNESS PROCESS	S STRANGER LEVEL	A ACQUAINTANCE LEVEL	F FRIEND LEVEL	E ETERNAL LEVEL
ACTIONS	Small acts of service and openness to listening	More serving and active listening	Regular serving, listening, and wondering	Regular serving, listening, wondering, and sharing
WORDS	"This is a practical way to show God's love."	"I want to get to know you better."	"I really care about you."	"Would you like to experience relationship with Jesus?"
GIFTS	Inexpensive and impersonal	Simple and related to our conversation	Special personal favorites	Personal and thought-provoking
TIME	Brief touch	Brief but more frequent touches	Regular access to your life	Significant connecting time
Golf	Driver	Long Iron	Short Iron	Putter
Gardening	Sow	Water	Tend	Harvest

SHARING YOUR OWN STORY

Yᴏu may not believe that your story is important, but God does. In fact, believe it or not, it is so unique that he has spent a lifetime training you to be the best person to tell it. Sharing what you have seen, heard, and experienced in your life has remarkable power—especially in this generation. We're not talking about canned, religious testimonies here but genuine, unrehearsed sharing about what has brought you to where you are in your life.

Unrehearsed doesn't necessarily mean unprepared. First Peter 3:14-15 says not to be frightened, but to set your heart on Christ and to "always be prepared to give an answer to everyone who asks you to give the reason for the hope that you have. But do this with gentleness and respect." Two things stand out in this passage: First, be ready when they ask. Expect that your serving, listening, and wondering will, in all likelihood, cause people to ask you to tell them why you choose to follow Christ. Second, be ready to tell your story with sensitivity and respect. Your relationship provides a context that allows you to relate your story to their experiences and beliefs.

How to Get Started

So how can you begin to put your story into words? You can write it down yourself or have a friend help by interviewing you. Use a pencil with a good eraser to fill in the form below as you respond to the questions. Don't worry if you can't fill in all the blanks. The purpose for telling and writing your story is to put it into a form that you can remember well enough to briefly share with anyone who may ask.

Pray that God will refresh your memory and help you crystallize your experiences into simple words. One way to do this is to ask God how he would tell your story. If you get any ideas, impressions, or word pictures, jot them down in the space provided below.

_____

_____

_____

_____

1. Outline your story in simple terms beginning with your family background, your beliefs, and your lifestyle before you began following Jesus as you do now.

Don't try to be profound, dramatic, or eloquent. Even if you came to Christ as a child, background, beliefs, and lifestyle are still part of your story.

Family Background: What was growing up like for you?

_____

_____

_____

Beliefs: What were your attitudes toward God, religion, and good and evil?

_____

_____

_____

Lifestyle: What were the most important things in your life?

_____

_____

_____

2. Explain any turning points (a crisis, an invitation, a relationship with another person, a response to a believing friend, reading the Bible, and so on) that caused you to consider committing your life to Jesus.

_____

_____

_____

_____

_____

3. Explain what brought you to the point of decision. Then describe the moment you asked Jesus to come into your life.

_____

_____

_____

_____

_____

4. Finally, honestly describe how your life has been changing since you started following Jesus.

_____

_____

_____

_____

_____

SAMPLE STORY: *Dave Ping*

When Dave prayed for God to refresh his memory and for God to help him tell his story, he immediately got an idea about how to tell it. "Even though my name, David, means 'beloved,' " he says, "I never really felt beloved as a child or as a teenager."

My Background

My parents were good people with big troubles in their lives. My dad was an alcoholic military officer who spent about nine months out of each year serving overseas in places like Korea and Vietnam. My mom was overwhelmed with the task of single-handedly taking care of kids and working full time to help pay all the bills. She read to us, helped us with our homework, led our Girl Scout and Cub Scout meetings, and even intermittently took us to church.

My Beliefs

Ever since I can remember, I'd heard that "God helps those who help themselves." I was sure that was in the Bible along with "Life is hard, so work hard and make the best of it." My mom always said that, if you're smart enough and work hard enough, you can accomplish anything you set your hand to. I thought that if I wanted anything, I had to work hard for it. Unfortunately the only thing I really wanted was love. And I worked hard to earn it from my mom, my dad, my teachers, and my friends, but however hard I tried, it never seemed to be enough. I did what I could to impress them, but my efforts always fell short.

My Lifestyle

When I was a teenager, we moved to Ohio where my dad took a job teaching ROTC at a small Midwestern university. When we got there, campus unrest and the drug culture were in full swing. As a rebellious teen, hungering to win friends and gain approval, I naturally gravitated to the longhaired, pot-smoking crowd. Some of the guys I hung out with were into buying drugs and alcohol and selling them to the college students. I mostly went along for the ride, but I slowly got more involved in the drug scene.

Considering Jesus

At school I was a "stoner." My friends and I were known drug-users, and all the upstanding students either avoided us or secretly bought drugs from us. Apart from other stoners, the only people who ever talked to me were Christians. They were dorky but kind of nice. Even though I made merciless fun of them, they kept on being friendly. Every once in a while, they would talk to me about God, and I would argue with them. But they didn't quit coming around. This was the closest thing to unconditional love I'd ever seen. I was secretly so interested when they talked about Jesus and God's love that I even started reading the Bible without telling anyone.

Why I Asked Jesus Into My Life

One day a girl named Merry asked me what I thought of Jesus, and I told her my latest theory about him. "He said, 'Blessed are the peacemakers for they will be called God's sons.' He was a pacifist and a peacemaker, so the establishment goons killed him. He never said he was God's Son or that he was the Messiah!"

Merry patiently told me I was mistaken and said I needed to read a booklet called Jesus and the Intellectual. I was sure I was right. So I said, "You show me in the Bible where Jesus said he was the Messiah, and I will read your little pamphlet or do anything else you want me to do." She calmly pulled a little New Testament from her backpack and proceeded to point out two places where Jesus clearly said he was both God's Son and the Messiah.

I took her booklet with every intention of throwing it away, but I put it in my pocket and walked off. I stopped off at an abandoned shack where my friends and I liked to smoke dope. I lit up a cigarette and read the booklet from cover to cover. By the time I was finished, I knew that if it was real I wanted the love of Jesus in my life. So I prayed, "God, if you exist, please come into my heart and change me."

My Life Since I Started Following Jesus

Something changed inside of me. Not right away, but gradually, I started to believe that God actually did love me, and I didn't have to do anything to earn it! Soon I found myself wanting to give love away to people without expecting or demanding anything in return. Through some pretty miraculous circumstances, I quit doing drugs and got involved in reaching out to other people, especially poor kids who'd never felt much love. My life's mission soon became sharing the love I've been given with as many people as possible.

If you don't have a checkered past like Dave, perhaps you will relate to Pam's journey into a deeper relationship with Jesus.

Sample Story: *Pam*

My Background

As the eldest of four girls in a military family, I'd learned responsibility, obedience, and respect. I was quiet and helpful in my neighborhood, church, Girl Scouts, and school. I learned to be other-centered. As the oldest kid in my neighborhood, I was a quiet leader, instigating things like a parade and festival to raise money for cancer. My parents expressed love openly. I lived by many "be considerate" rules like never saying "shut up," helping others without being asked, and doing what I was told. Family life included lots of humor, memorable family vacations...and discipline. Life was basically good and secure.

Neither my sisters nor I got into the drug scene or even cigarette smoking, for that matter. My sisters married pretty much right after high school and started families. My journey was different.

A Turning Point

I remember the moment when, in my sophomore year in high school, I became aware that I was hungering for "something more." As I rinsed shampoo out of my hair one morning in the shower, I thought, "Is this all there is? Get up, get ready for school, come home, do homework, go to bed. Only to get up the next morning and start all over again. What's the point?" Life seemed pointless.

That same year, I went on a retreat with our church youth group where leaders, who were not of my church denomination, spoke of strange things like giving your heart to Jesus and being baptized in the Spirit. Even though it broke all my internal rules to ask for something for myself, I agreed to let them pray with me to receive Jesus as Savior. I cried a lot that night (I don't know why). The next morning, everything seemed to look crisper...and I felt somehow lighter.

My Life With Christ

After that, most of what I learned about following Christ came from reading books by people like Corrie Ten Boom, David Wilkerson, and Nicky Cruz. They told many stories about how God miraculously directed people in making big decisions. When I went away to college, I had no idea what major to choose. I started with an undecided major because I expected God would tell me what to do—but he never did.

I spent over a year asking God for direction and dutifully waiting for three unmistakable confirmations before acting. One day as I was praying, I got a distinct impression that God was telling me that I wasn't trusting him or myself. I'd been trying to go by the book, struggling to clock at least thirty minutes a day praying and reading

Scripture. But God seemed to be gently admonishing me, saying, "Pam, just be with me!" He wanted a relationship with me. That opened a whole new world.

God started teaching me how to discover and to be myself. He didn't want to tell me what to do—he wanted me to choose for myself and to take pleasure in becoming the person he'd made me to be. An important piece of this journey was learning to face and even value my anger. I learned that God not only cherishes parts of me that I like, but even treats my anger as precious. This realization opened the way for me to walk in healthier, more honest relationships. Eventually, when I was thirty-six, he gave me enough of myself to marry my best friend and lay ministry partner, Dave.

Over the years, the Lord has done more than give me a rich new life of my own; he has helped me to share what he gave me with people all over the United States and in places like Scandinavia, Cuba, and India. You see, good girls need Jesus too!

Your Story

Your story has its own special power. Take the opportunity to think it through and be ready to share it with Christians and pre-Christians alike as they ask about your life. You'll be amazed how God can use your life to spur questions and to provide a clearer picture of what faith in Jesus looks like.

Endnotes

1. C.S. Lewis, *George MacDonald: An Anthology* (San Francisco: Harper SF, 2001).

2. "Even though you have ten thousand guardians in Christ, you do not have many fathers, for in Christ Jesus I became your father through the gospel." (1 Corinthians 4:15).

3. Although they get some bad press for how they've sometimes been misused, variations on The Roman Road approach and Campus Crusade for Christ's Four Spiritual Laws are classic tools Doug, Dave, and Steve have used for helping countless people who were ready to make a decision. Approximately 1.5 billion copies of the "Four Spiritual Laws Booklet" have been printed, and they are available in just about every language. For information about the four laws, contact www.ccci.org.

CHAPTER 10

An Arsonist's Guide to EVANGELISM

"God not only offers forgiveness, reconciliation, and healing, but wants to lift up these gifts as a source of joy for all who witness them."
—HENRI J.M. NOUWEN,
*The Return of
the Prodigal Son*

"Do not put out the Spirit's fire."
—1 THESSALONIANS 5:19

United States Fire Administration statistics show that one out of every four fires is caused by arson, accounting for some half a million fires and $3 billion in direct property damage each year. When people intentionally set fires, lives are lost and property is destroyed, but when God ignites spiritual fires, hearts are filled with love and lives are saved.

Exodus 3:2-3 tells us how the angel of the Lord appeared to Moses in the flames of a burning bush. Moses was fascinated because although the bush was clearly on fire, it wasn't damaged and it didn't burn up. Moses was irresistibly drawn toward the sight, thinking, "I've got to check this out!" There's a heavenly quality to God's presence that piques our interest and tugs on our hearts. That's why, whenever a person or a congregation is truly on fire with God's love, people will come from miles around just to watch them "burn."

Whenever a person or a congregation is truly on fire with God's love, people will come from miles around just to watch them "burn."

Nothing is more exciting or scarier than fire. We're drawn toward it, and yet we have an instinctive fear of getting burned. The good news is that when God sets the fires of evangelism loose in your church, they won't damage its people or consume scarce resources. On the contrary, these fires will bring more light, more hope, and more resources through the door than you ever dreamed possible. The fire isn't like another program that sucks up all your top-notch volunteers and piles more burdens on the backs of already overburdened staff. If it's God's fire, it ignites the most unlikely people to step forward and lead. They become *God's arsonists*, enflaming and inspiring your congregation to previously unimagined accomplishments!

We usually don't connect arson with something positive, but setting hearts on fire to reach others for Christ is a very positive thing indeed. Though God's fires don't burn people out, they do need spiritual fuel. The fuel God requires is a volatile mixture of irresistible attitudes that inflame people to carry out godly actions.

Fuelish Attitudes

Fuelish attitudes are five ways of thinking that ignite ordinary church members with a passion for introducing their family, friends, neighbors, and complete strangers into life-changing relationships with Jesus Christ. They naturally blend the Lord's great commandment[1] and his great commission.[2] They combine love and truth in an amazingly attractive way. So what are these five fuels?

The Fuel of Kindness

The kindness that flows from the heart of God is truly irresistible. Colossians 3:12 tells us that as God's "chosen people," we are to *"clothe [ourselves]* with compassion, kindness, humility, gentleness and patience" (emphasis added). Clothing ourselves means wrapping ourselves up in God's love for anyone in need—anyone who is hungry, hurting, or lonely. It means adopting outward-focused, other-centered habits of thinking and relating to replace the self-absorbed, me-first consumerism that's dominated our culture for more than half a century. Perhaps instead of making decisions based on the latest marketing demographics, it would be good to find guidance from the simple prayer Francis of Assisi taught his followers way back in the thirteenth century:

> *Lord,*
> *make me an instrument of your peace.*
> *Where there is hatred, let me sow love;*
> *where there is injury, pardon;*
> *where there is doubt, faith;*
> *where there is despair, hope;*
> *where there is darkness, light;*
> *where there is sadness, joy.*
> *O Divine Master,*
> *grant that I may not so much seek*
> *to be consoled, as to console;*
> *to be understood, as to understand;*
> *to be loved, as to love.*
> *For it is in giving that we receive;*
> *it is in pardoning that we are pardoned;*
> *and it is in dying*
> *that we are born to eternal life.*

Taking the focus off of ourselves and putting it on God and the needs of others is amazingly fuelish! Here's the story of how one church has started living out Saint Francis' prayer.

The Abbotsford Vineyard Church in British Columbia, Canada, had gone through the wringer. The church had barely survived a church split, and people had continued leaving in great numbers throughout a couple of years.

By the time the remnant who'd lived through these dark days asked Terry Lamb to come and serve as their new pastor, the vision they'd originally followed had been ground into the dirt and almost completely lost. Terry felt that God might be calling him there, but he had significant reservations. He agreed to come and see how things went, but he wasn't willing to sign up for a long-term commitment.

After a couple of years of rebuilding, Terry met Steve and invited him to come to Abbotsford and share his vision for reaching out to the community through acts of kindness. What Steve found when he got there was a little discouraging. Steve reports:

> *The forty people assembled before me were all "walking wounded." They were beat-up and depressed, and they didn't have much positive expectation of what God had in mind for them. After a couple of days of learning new ways to reach out to their city with God's kindness, they became increasingly eager and excited about doing an outreach.*
>
> *That first day's outreach was a little rough. The soft drinks we gave away were warm, and dozens of our free Popsicles melted before we could hand them out. Some of the church people weren't mindful of the traffic patterns: They irritated some motorists and caused a few minor traffic jams. But in spite of all of the mistakes, they were pumped up! They loved the way people responded to their little gestures of kindness. Focusing outward gave them a much-needed break from worrying about their congregation's problems. I went home with a sense that we'd ignited a little spark of hope in Abbotsford, but I had no idea how powerfully and rapidly it would catch that city on fire.*
>
> *The Saturday after the first outreach, the group got together and did it again. It was even more enjoyable the second time! Soon members of*

the group started inviting other churches to join them on their weekend outreaches to share the kindness of Christ with the community. As other congregations showed up, the group learned from their mistakes and got better at showing kindness. Four years later, tens of thousands have received their little touches of kindness. Instead of licking their wounds and replaying past tragedies, the people of the Abbotsford Vineyard Church have been actively serving, listening, wondering, and sharing Christ. They've connected with strangers, acquaintances, friends, and fellow Christians from all over town. Sparks of simple kindness have been spreading all over, igniting a roaring fire.

That broken, limping church Terry stepped in to lead has all but disappeared. In its place, he and the formerly depressed faithful members now lead a growing congregation of dynamic Christ-followers that attracts about 350 people to worship each weekend. Together with the local ministerial association, they've also founded a movement called Love [your city] that's inspiring outreach, worship, and cooperation. The movement has already spread to churches in fifteen cities all over the country.[3] Does kindness work to change hearts of church people? You bet!

The Fuel of Fun

One reason lots of people stay away from church is that it's no fun. Too many people think that, if they choose to follow Christ, all the fun will be over. Nothing could be further from the truth. In fact, one of our favorite sayings is "Where the Spirit of the Lord is, there is fun!" In Abbotsford the people quickly realized that giving freely with no strings attached is incredibly fun. Not only can people of all ages and abilities participate, they can have big fun in the process. The following letter was received by the organizers of a recent kindness outreach.

> *Giving freely with no strings attached is incredibly fun.*

Hey...that was sooooo much fun! Can we do that EVERY Saturday??? Even our four-year-old got in on the action. We were down by the freeway on Sumas Way and Marshall Road handing out soft drinks, and she was such a great big help putting the cards on the cans and pushing the button for the light to turn red that she wasn't in any danger on the road at all! God even made sure that the weather held out for us...the downpour didn't start until we were all through. Thanks again for the experience.

God bless,

Hugh, Carla & Cassidy

The best kind of fun is fun that allows us to care for people's real needs and opens hearts to God. Another letter the Abbotsford organizers received shows how small things that were genuinely fun to do transformed one family's world in a big way.

I just wanted to tell you thank you for what you are doing. I am just a nobody...going through severe crisis in my life, single with two children. I took my son to his soccer game today and your group was there. Let me give you some history first...I have been living day to day trying to just make it through the day and being happy if my children got one full meal. This morning I had to explain to them that once again I didn't have anything to give them for breakfast. They understood, but I knew they were very hungry.

When we got to the soccer game at Abby School, your group was there having a free pancake breakfast and car wash. My children were both so excited to have a full meal, and when a young boy handed me a soda and said, "Jesus loves you," I just about broke into tears. It may have seemed menial to some, but I have to tell you...there is no way that I can tell you what kind of faith you have restored to my life. I guess God is real and does watch over even the worst of us. I have not gone to church in fifteen years and have always been bitter at churches, but this one simple pancake breakfast has made me change my whole way of thinking. I will be seeking out a church that I feel comfortable going to. So thank you from myself and my children.

What a huge victory for God! How humbling that someone in such real need and so bitter toward the church could be moved just by getting a free pancake breakfast and a can of soda. The whole experience cost only a few Canadian dollars, but how much was it worth in God's economy?

The Fuel of Outrageous Generosity

Jesus tells us in Matthew 6:33 that those who seek first the kingdom of God and his righteousness need not worry about where their food, drink, or clothing will come from. Our heavenly Father knows that we need these things and they will be provided. What an outrageous proclamation! What a frighteningly exciting idea—if it is genuinely true. But we'll never know if it's true or not unless we step out and try a little outrageous generosity.

Dale attended the Abbotsford Vineyard Church, but he had vowed to Terry that he would never participate in kindness outreach. He simply saw no value in it. However, one Saturday he grudgingly showed up for an outreach. He and a friend tried their hands at the hot dog giveaway and found, to their utter surprise, that they absolutely loved serving hot dogs for free to show people the love of Christ.

As Dale was grilling and giving out hot dogs with a big smile on his face, a single, pregnant mom approached him with four small kids in tow. In a thick Spanish accent, she let him know that she was extremely grateful for the free food because her husband had abandoned her and her kids only the day before. Until that day, Dale had never clearly heard the voice of the Lord speak to him, but he believes that at that moment God told him to give her all the money in his wallet. Usually that wouldn't have been a big deal, but he had just come from the bank and had much more cash than usual. Nevertheless, Dale obeyed the prompting and gave it all away. Tears filled the woman's eyes, and she was completely speechless with gratefulness.

Today Dale *loves* kindness outreaches. He stores the hot dog cart in his own garage, and Terry says he won't let anyone else touch it! He *owns* this outreach. And what of the Hispanic lady? She hasn't yet given her life to Christ, but she and her children are fixtures at a local church that offers Spanish language services. If the wondering questions she's asking are any indication, she's well on her way to the green.

Another example of generosity happened a few years ago as the people of Vineyard Community Church in Cincinnati were in the middle of a fundraising campaign because they had outgrown their building. The pastors and worship teams were doing six identical services per weekend, and the building was still bursting at the seams. At that time, they needed about $1 million to purchase the property where their new building would stand. This was a huge amount of money for them in those days. Steve tells what happened:

> *We'd been teaching our people from 2 Corinthians 9:6: "Whoever sows sparingly will also reap sparingly, and whoever sows generously will also reap generously." It seemed like a pretty good text for fundraising, but suddenly it occurred to us that perhaps we should practice what we were preaching. Maybe the best way to get our needs met would be to step out to meet the needs of someone else in a similar situation, so we looked around our city for another church that was also in the middle of a building campaign.*
>
> *We found one—a predominantly African-American church that had nothing to do with the Vineyard movement. After taking up a special offering at all six of our services, we invited that church's pastor and his wife to come to our Wednesday evening worship. We didn't give them any warning about what we were planning; we just told them we wanted to pray for them. After praying, we told the pastor we had a gift to encourage his church in its building program. He told us later that he assumed it was for a couple of hundred dollars. We were all overjoyed when he opened the envelope and saw that it contained a check made out to his church for $36,500. Now that was fun! Our people applauded for several minutes and then broke into spontaneous praise and worship that just wouldn't stop.*

From a human perspective, it was outrageous to give away so much money when we desperately needed every penny we could scrape together for our new property. But we were seeking first God's kingdom and relying on God for the rest. We were sowing generously in full expectation that we'd reap generously. We were also modeling the kind of faith we were asking of our congregation. We were pouring fuel on their hearts and watching them catch fire with faith and generosity. When we concluded our campaign, we had not only all the money we needed, but many more generous people who were looking outward and asking themselves, "Who else can we help?"

The Fuel of Humility

Another attitude that allows the fires of evangelism to burn brightly is humility. Big things happen when we operate with simple modesty. Whenever we allow our evangelism to become overly identified with any person other than Jesus or any church other than his church, we miss the point. When all the stories end up being about how cool we are instead of how cool God is, we start to get caught up in a peculiar form of idolatry that Doug calls fake-ianity.

One way to keep the humility factor high is to invite lots of other churches to participate in outreach with you. This way it's clear to everyone that you aren't just can-vassing for new members to build up your church's reputation or budget. It really *is* all about Jesus. The people from Abbotsford Vineyard began doing this right away. They don't trumpet the church name in their out-reaches; instead they go under the name Love Abbotsford and involve anywhere from fifty to one hundred people from sev-
eral local churches in monthly outreaches. They regularly send the people they reach to other churches that are closer to where they live or provide a better fit for people's particular needs. They also regularly share stories about their mistakes and failures and get

especially excited when they can show how God turns even their biggest blunders into successes.

Humility means measuring our successes and failures according to God's standard. Since nobody is kinder or more honest than he is, and because his perfect love casts out fear and condemnation, humility is remarkably attractive and refreshing. It means owning up to the fact that, as Dave loves to say, "We're all Bozos on this bus!" The only raw material God uses to build his kingdom is broken, fallible people. Most pre-Christians already know we're as messed up, or in many cases, worse than they are. They've just been waiting for us to give up our hypocrisy and admit it. Let's shock them by getting real about our faults while being genuinely loving at the same time.

The only raw material God uses to build his kingdom is broken, fallible people.

The Fuel of Prayer and Worship

At the Abbotsford Vineyard, worship and prayer drive everything these days. Sure, the people reach out in lots of tangible ways all of the time. They serve, listen, practice active wondering, and share what this book talks about. But they also constantly acknowledge their dependence upon the power of prayer.

They pray before they do outreach, as they practice outreach, and after the outreach. Whether we're doing a large-group outreach or having an intimate conversation between two or three friends, not much happens if God doesn't show up. If we invite and welcome God's presence, look out! He'll work in mysterious ways his wonders to perform!

The Abbotsford church began to grow deep in worship before it began to grow out in numbers. The Holy Spirit called the people to get past the shallowness that came naturally and to move toward something deeper and more dynamic. They learned new ways of expressing their love to God through music and the creative arts. They quickly discovered that worship couldn't be confined to the four walls of the church—it had to be loosed upon the greater community. Worship celebrations popped up in local parks through the talents of dancers, actors, singers, and musicians. Not only were those with talents able to express themselves, but they drew the city into the act of worship.

We believe that when people really catch on fire with the Spirit, they'll always want to evangelize. Theologians have suggested many signs that show the life and presence of the Holy Spirit in a person, but we believe that an almost uncontrollable desire to evangelize is the best indicator of the Spirit's presence! Hungering and thirsting to share what we've been given is the natural byproduct of a life that is lived moment by moment with God.

GETTING RID OF ASBESTOS ATTITUDES

Church leaders who would love to ignite their congregations to reach out to their communities often encounter internal problems that inhibit enthusiasm and quench bold actions. The following five *asbestos attitudes* encourage us to spend lots of time sitting around thinking, reading books, and even preaching about outreach, without ever getting around to mobilizing our people to act effectively.

Attitude of Fear

A wise man once said, "Truth separated from experience remains eternally in the realm of doubt." Evangelism is frightening because it is uncharted territory for the vast majority of people in our churches. They may understand the theory and even know what they should do, but their heads are still filled with fearful questions like "What if I try it and fail?" and "What if I reach out and people judge and reject me?" or "What if I reach out and nothing great happens? What if someone asks me a question I can't answer?" Unrealistic demands and unpleasant experiences with evangelism just intensify these fears. That's why it's important to introduce people to evangelistic experiences safely and in stages that are appropriate to their level of spiritual maturity.

Doug says a lot of the evangelism training he sees reminds him of a traumatic experience he had as a small child learning how to dive at the swimming pool:

Our instructor thought that the best way to get us over our fear of diving was to make us go off the high dive first. He was a tough, drill-sergeant kind of guy who seemed to take pleasure in mocking and humiliating the kids who hesitated. When I climbed to the top of the ladder, my fear of being ridiculed by my instructor in front of my friends was greater than my fear of heights and drowning—so I dived off like everybody else. Unfortunately, I hit with a giant belly-smacker. I eventually learned how to dive, but to this day I still don't enjoy it.

That experience soured me on diving the same way lots of people get soured on sharing their faith. The way lots of people get their feet wet in evangelism is the emotional equivalent to going blindfolded off a high dive. We send them out knocking on strangers' doors, armed with Bible tracts and a forty-five-minute pep talk about their responsibility to go win souls. Sometimes we use peer pressure to shame them into it. Even if the Holy Spirit prevails and the outcome is positive, many will remember the fear and embarrassment of the experience long after they forget the positives.

Some fear is unavoidable, but if we want people to be highly motivated to repeat an experience, we must give them easily doable steps through which they're likely to have fun, gain know-how, and taste the pleasure of success. Kindness outreach is a great way to get started because it's low-threat and high-grace. We could tell hundreds of stories just like the ones we've told already about how God showed up and changed somebody's life when an inexperienced, first-time evangelist gave a can of soda or a balloon in Christ's name.

Once people have experienced the simple "swimming lessons" of kindness, they want to dive into the necessary lessons of listening. When they're consistently connecting in real relationships and naturally want more, we teach them active wondering.

Suddenly they're having real conversations with people about life and God, and they're ready for the high dive of sharing.

They're no longer afraid. The questions that kept them paralyzed before have been answered in the show-and-tell process along the way. They're so excited you couldn't keep them away from the pool if you tried! We wonder if this is how, as 1 John 4:18 says, "Perfect love drives out fear." Instead of expecting failure and condemnation, we come to expect the joy and passion of God showing up and using what we've learned to help others discover his love.

"Big Deal" Attitude

Another asbestos attitude that can snuff the fires of evangelism is thinking of outreach only in terms of one-time, "big-deal" events instead of as a continuous and ongoing effort. Many who have tried one or two big servant evangelism projects don't understand why the interest that was so high at first fades away after a while. It loses its appeal if it becomes an every-now-and-then kind of thing that *somebody else* is doing instead of a daily activity that's part of following Christ.

Special projects and crusade-type missions can foster a picture of evangelism as a short-term big push. People begin thinking in harvest-only terms and forget about the daily relational work of sowing, watering, and tending. They forget about the constant process of raising people up to find Jesus, follow him, and reproduce themselves in ministry. It's as if we get the idea into our heads that we can be fabulously successful just by going to work once or twice a year. It sounds too good to be true—and it is.

One-shot, big-deal attitudes can creep into our personal relationships, our marriages, and our parenting. This happens when we try to replace daily faithfulness in little things with grand tokens and gestures. Doug tells about how he was able to give a special anniversary present to his wife Martha:

I made reservations for a bed and breakfast and a romantic river cruise. I also got great tickets for a Cincinnati Reds game and talked the guy who runs the JumboTron at the stadium into printing out my romantic happy anniversary message in huge twenty-five-foot letters three different times during the game. She was excited when she finally realized that she was the Martha mentioned on the screen.

I thought this big display of my affection would have a huge impact on her, and I admit that I hoped to get lots of marital mileage out of it. I was counting on being treated like a king for the next few weeks. The sad thing I found out is that staying happily married is much more than grand gestures; it's taking out the trash, talking through our disagreements, and parenting our kids. Grand gestures are just the icing, not the cake.

It's the same way with sharing your faith. Big splash events are fun and exciting, but they're no substitute for the hundreds of day-to-day actions that say "I love you" or "God loves you." If tokenism is the only love we show, the fire quickly sputters and goes out.

Me-First Attitude

Quite a few churches have breathed in the me-first attitude of the baby boomer generation, and it has become a hidden part of everything they do. Only brave leaders dare challenge the epidemic of self-centeredness and smug self-satisfaction that leads to ignoring the needs and hurts of others. Spiritual consumerism is all about me and mine—my comfort, my convenience, and my self-esteem are the primary concerns of the church.

For the last seven years, Dave has done an exercise at the beginning of his seminars for pastors and leaders. He asks leaders to define what overwhelming success would look like if God had his way with their churches. People's lists usually paint an inspiring picture of a place where people are constantly giving and receiving God's love and truth. In that picture, lives are being changed and whole cities are being transformed.

Dave's second question is "How do you think an average person who attends your church would define congregational success?" At that point, the answers change dramatically. The focus switches to impressive facilities, full parking lots, big budgets, great preaching, exciting music, and professional-quality programs to meet every type of need. None of these things is bad, *they're just not the main event.*

For a church, the main event must reflect the servant heart of Jesus. That's why for the last several years Steve has been taking teams of Cincinnati suburbanites to the dumps of Mexico City to serve the families who make their living by picking through the trash. The teams offer medical, dental, and optical care in the name of Jesus. They show Christ's love to impoverished children by hugging them, braiding their hair, and simply playing games with them.

For a church, the main event must reflect the servant heart of Jesus.

These middle-class participants from Cincinnati see the tragedy of Mexico City's thousands of street children—mostly runaways—who spend their entire day inhaling (huffing) paint thinner to stay high. The teams care for these street people, serving food and conversing through translators. In short, they become hope distributors for those who've fallen so far out of the parade of life they can't even hear the music anymore.

People who take these trips to Mexico City always come back changed. They do a lot of good for the poor at the dumpsites and for the needy who are addicted to substances. But the ones who come to do the changing are always the ones most changed; the greatest good always happens to those who do the giving. They're always radically changed. That's the way of God's kingdom.

Apathy Attitude

If we—Steve, Dave, and Doug—had our druthers, the three of us would like to set up a giant field trip. We'd take all the church leaders and ordinary Christians we could find to Somerset, Pennsylvania, the place where nine miners were trapped 240 feet

down in the darkness of a flooded mine. It's a place where everything came to a screeching halt at 9 p.m. on Wednesday, July 24,
2002, when miners accidentally drilled into an abandoned tunnel
and released 50 million gallons of water, flooding the mine and
trapping the nine men inside.

When the people above ground realized what was happening,
everything stopped being normal. All thoughts and prayers
turned to finding ways to save those nine men. Authorities organized all the resources they could find. People came from near and
far, bringing the latest technology and equipment. They used a
GPS satellite to pinpoint the location of the trapped men. The rescuers then drilled narrow shafts and lowered listening devices
down to where they thought the miners might be. Following a
series of faint tapping sounds, the rescuers eventually located the
men. They were huddled together in a small air pocket, fighting
off the effects of hypothermia as the waters continued to rise
around them. Once they were discovered, around-the-clock
drilling began. Six special diamond-tipped drills and twelve aux-
iliary air compressors were brought in and put to work on the site,
boring a hole large enough to bring out the men.

Millions of dollars, hundreds of workmen, and countless
prayers all came into play during this seventy-seven-hour rescue
drama. Millions watched on TV and waited for news, all for one
simple reason: Men, human beings just like us, were lost and
dying. No one suggested that this effort was too difficult or
expensive. We wanted to give them a chance to live. We wanted
them to see the sun and to breathe the fresh air again.

Every one of us has a special part to play.

The reason we'd like to take busloads of fellow
Christians to Somerset is to remind the church that
people's lives are *still* on the line. People whom God
loves and whom we love are *still* struggling in the
dark. God has commissioned each of us to do our part in the rescue
effort. We need to realize the urgency and muster all the creativity,
skill, wisdom, and teamwork we can bring together. The task may
seem insurmountable, but this is not a time to be apathetic.

This is not a guilt trip; it's a wake-up call. Every one of us has a special part to play. Each can serve and listen and ask wondering questions. Each can share the little spark of light we've been given. If we work together and don't give up, many more people will walk in the light and breathe the fresh, clean air of faith in Jesus Christ!

Strike a Match!

One of the favorite kindness outreach projects at Vineyard Community Church in Cincinnati is giving away free books of matches to people in bars, restaurants, and gas stations. Each book has the church's logo on the front, a map to the church, service times, and the church's phone number. Over the past several years the church has given away tens of thousands of matchbooks to smokers in the Cincinnati area. Steve tells of going into a bar to hand out free matches:

As we walked in, the bartender took a look at us and snarled, "Whatever you have, we don't want any."

"OK," I said, "I just thought you might want to have some Christian matches. They're absolutely free!"

"What? Christian matches?"

"Yeah, matches for your customers who smoke."

"But I thought that church people hated people who smoke."

"No, you've got it all wrong. We love people who smoke."

"You're messing with me!"

"No kidding! We went out and printed thousands of packets of matches just for customers like yours to show you God's love in a practical way."

"Well, in that case, we'll take a bunch of matches."

By that time in the conversation, the entire clientele of the bar had gathered around and was leaning toward us to hear more clearly. After all, it wasn't every day that someone came into the bar to offer Christian matches.

We hope that every time a person strikes one of these matches he or she will realize, "Hey, those guys aren't against people like me. They'll love me whether I smoke or not. Maybe there's a place for me at that church."

Isn't this what evangelism is really all about? Wouldn't you like to set your church on fire? Perhaps it's time to start liberally pouring on the fuel of Christ's kindness, his joy, his outrageous generosity, his humility, his attitude of prayer and worship! Soak your church, your neighborhood, your friends, your children, and your city in it. Saturate yourself in God's love. Serve, listen, wonder, share! God's just waiting to strike the match—and to help you burn with an irresistible fire that can be seen for miles around. People who need to know Jesus will be drawn toward the sight, thinking, "Wow, I've got to check this out!"

ENDNOTES

1. " 'Love the Lord your God with all your heart and with all your soul and with all your strength and with all your mind'; and, 'Love your neighbor as yourself' " (Luke 10:27).

2. "Go and make disciples of all nations, baptizing them in the name of the Father and of the Son and of the Holy Spirit, and teaching them to obey everything I have commanded you" (Matthew 28:19-20).

3. Check out their Web site at www.loveyourcity.com.

BOOKS

Clegg, Tom, and Warren Bird. *Lost in America: How You and Your Church Can Impact the World Next Door.* Loveland, CO: Group Publishing, 2001.

Cloud, Henry, and John Townsend. *How People Grow: What the Bible Reveals About Personal Growth.* Grand Rapids, MI: Zondervan, 2001.

Downs, Tim. *Finding Common Ground: How to Communicate With Those Outside the Christian Community…While We Still Can.* Chicago: Moody Press, 1999.

Dreisbach, Bruce Roberts. *The Jesus Plan: Breaking Through Barriers to Introduce the People You Know to the God You Love.* Colorado Springs: WaterBrook Press, 2002.

Gallup, George, Jr., and Timothy Jones. *The Next American Spirituality: Finding God in the Twenty-First Century.* Colorado Springs: Cook Communications Ministries, 2000.

Gary Sweeten, Dave Ping, and Anne Clippard, *Listening for Heaven's Sake: Building Healthy Relationships With God, Self and Others.* Cincinnati: Teleios Publications, 1993.

Grenz, Stanley J. *A Primer on Postmodernism.* Grand Rapids, MI: William B. Eerdmans Publishing Co., 1996.

Hunter, George G. III. *Radical Outreach: Recovery of Apostolic Ministry and Evangelism.* Nashville: Abingdon Press, 2003.

Hunter, George G. III. *The Celtic Way of Evangelism: How Christianity Can Reach the West…Again,* Nashville: Abingdon Press, 2000.

Hybels, Bill, and Mark Mittelberg. *Becoming a Contagious Christian: Communicating Your Faith in a Style That Fits You.* Grand Rapids, MI: Zondervan, 1995.

Johnson, Ronald W. *How Will They Hear If We Don't Listen?* Nashville: Broadman & Holman Publishers, 1994.

Manning, Brennan. *The Ragamuffin Gospel.* Sisters, OR: Multnomah Publishers, Inc., 2000.

McIntosh, Gary L. *One Church, Four Generations: Understanding and Reaching All Ages in Your Church.* Grand Rapids, MI: Baker Books, 2002.

McLaren, Brian D. *A New Kind of Christian: A Tale of Two Friends on a Spiritual Journey.* San Francisco: Jossey-Bass, 2001.

McLaren, Brian D. *Finding Faith: A Self-Discovery Guide for Your Spiritual Quest.* Grand Rapids, MI: Zondervan, 1999.

McLaren, Brian D. *More Ready Than You Realize: Evangelism as Dance in the Postmodern Matrix.* Grand Rapids, MI: Zondervan, 2002.

Pollard, Nick. *Evangelism Made Slightly Less Difficult: How to Interest People Who Aren't Interested.* Downers Grove, IL: InterVarsity Press, 1997.

Putnam, Robert D. *Bowling Alone: The Collapse and Revival of American Community.* New York: Simon & Schuster, 2000.

Rainer, Thom S. *Surprising Insights From the Unchurched and Proven Ways to Reach Them.* Grand Rapids, MI: Zondervan, 2001.

Richardson, Rick. *Evangelism Outside the Box: New Ways to Help People Experience the Good News.* Downers Grove, IL: InterVarsity Press, 2000.

Sjogren, Steve, and Janie Sjogren. *101 Ways to Help People in Need.* Colorado Springs: NavPress, 2001.

Sjogren, Steve, and Rob Lewin. *Community of Kindness: A Refreshing New Approach to Planting and Growing a Church.* Ventura, CA: Regal Books, 2003.

Sjogren, Steve. *101 Ways to Reach Your Community.* Colorado Springs: NavPress, 2001.

Sjogren, Steve. *Conspiracy of Kindness: A Refreshing New Approach to Sharing the Love of Jesus With Others.* Ann Arbor, MI: Vine Books, 1993, 2003.

Sjogren, Steve. *Seeing Beyond Church Walls: Action Plans for Touching Your Community.* Loveland, CO: Group Publishing, Inc., 2002.

Sjogren, Steve. *The Perfectly Imperfect Church: Redefining the "Ideal" Church.* Loveland, CO: Group Publishing, 2002.

Sweet, Leonard. *Post-Modern Pilgrims: First Century Passion for the 21st Century World.* Nashville: Broadman & Holman Publishers, 2000.

Tuttle, Robert G. *Can We Talk? Sharing Your Faith in a Pre-Christian World.* Nashville: Abingdon Press, 1999.

CURRICULUM

Becoming a Contagious Christian: Communicating Your Faith in a Style That Fits You. Mittelberg, Mark, Lee Strobel, and Bill Hybels. Grand Rapids, MI: Zondervan, 1995.

Irresistible Evangelism Training Kit. Steve Sjogren, Dave Ping, and Doug Pollock, Cincinnati: Equipping Ministries Intl., 2004.

This kit will help you lead Christian adults and teens past their fears and negative preconceptions of evangelism to discover lots of safe, natural ways to share new life in Jesus. The kit contains eight high-impact, fifty-five-minute learning sessions; interactive discussion starter and teaching DVD, step-by-step leaders guide, high quality participant handouts. Available at www.equipmin.org, or call 1-800-EMI-GROW.

Listening for Heaven's Sake: Building Trust and Openness. Dave Ping and Anne Clippard. Cincinnati: Equipping Ministries Intl.

A ten-hour interactive training for creating an attractive, caring atmosphere in your church. Onsite training and video-assisted instructor's kit available from Equipping Ministries. 1-800-EMI-GROW or www.equipmin.org.

SPEAKERS

If you are interested in having Steve Sjogren, Dave Ping, Doug Pollock, or another highly equipped and gifted presenter come to your church to speak on irresistible evangelism, please contact us at 1-800-EMI-GROW or 513-742-1100.

VIDEOS

Sjogren, Steve. *Introduction to Servant Evangelism.*

This thirteen-minute video is the perfect way to introduce pastors, lay leaders, friends, and colleagues to this wonderfully practical and powerful outreach model called servant evangelism. Available at www.servantevangelism.com.

Sjogren, Steve. *Servant Evangelism for Scaredy-cats.*

A one-hour video: Teaching the basics of servant evangelism at Starbucks. Available at www.servantevangelism.com.

Sjogren, Steve. *Servant Evangelism Seminar.*

The message of servant evangelism is creating a wave of excitement across North America and around the world as churches grasp the simple but powerful evangelistic effects of showing God's love in practical ways. Available at www.servantevangelism.com.

Irresistible Evangelism
OUTREACH TRAINING KIT

Everything you need to equip ordinary people to share God's love and have great fun doing it

Irresistible Evangelism is now available in an interactive course that is effective with groups of all sizes, from intimate small-group gatherings to Sunday school classes or large retreats with hundreds of participants. The kit includes everything you need* to lead Christian adults and teens past their fears and negative preconceptions of evangelism to discover lots of safe, natural ways to share new life in Jesus.

You get all of this:

- eight 55-minute video-assisted learning sessions that are compelling, practical, and genuinely easy to lead

- a step-by-step Leader Guide with high-quality, reproducible participant handouts for each session

- a DVD filled with thought-provoking discussion starters, live-action interviews, and great teaching

- flexible schedules that allow you to adapt to meet the special needs and time requirements of your group

- lots of practical Ideas for promoting and following up your training experience

- a sample copy of *Irresistible Evangelism*

Irresistible Evangelism texts are required for each participant and may be purchased at generous group discounts.

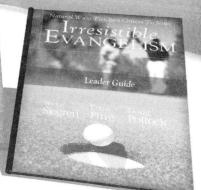

Order today from
Equipping Ministries International
by calling **1-800-364-4769**
or order on-line at **www.equippingministries.org**